They Called It Holy

שער הקדושה ואגרת הקודש

They Called It Holy

Physical and Spiritual Intimacy Between Man and Woman

The Holy Gate
by Ravad
(Rabbenu Avraham ben David of Posquierre)

The Holy Letter
attributed to Ramban
(Rabbenu Moshe ben Nachman)

Hebrew / English

Translated and Edited by
MOSHE DAVID KUHR, MD

Urim Publications
Jerusalem · New York

They Called It Holy
Physical and Spiritual Intimacy Between Man and Woman
The Holy Gate by Ravad
and *The Holy Letter* attributed to Ramban

Hebrew text of *The Holy Gate – Shaar Hakedusha* from the book *Ba'alei Hanefesh* of the Ravad (prepared and edited from a unique manuscript by Rabbi Yosef David Kapach, and published by Mossad Harav Kook), used with permission.

Hebrew text of *The Holy Letter – Iggeret Hakodesh* attributed to the Ramban, courtesy of Sefaria.

Translated and Edited by Moshe David Kuhr, MD

Typeset by Juliet Tresgallo

Printed in Israel
First Edition
ISBN 978-965-524-386-4

Urim Publications
P.O. Box 52287
Jerusalem 9152102, Israel
www.UrimPublications.com

Cataloging-in-Publication data is available from the Library of Congress.

מוסדות אור שמח מרכז טננבאום

MICHTAV BRACHA

Nissan 5784

WITHIN THE CONFINES of the Jewish tradition, marital intimacy and indeed sexuality as a whole were normally not matters of public discussion. Rooted in the time-honored values of *tzniyut*, this laudable reticence led to an unfortunate and erroneous conclusion that Judaism regarded marital relations as somehow dirty, improper or shameful, and something to be avoided. At best, it could be tolerated as a concession to human weakness, but ideally, celibacy would be the preferred holier state. In reality, nothing could be further from the truth. Intentional celibacy is actually sinful; marriage is an elevated state of spirituality, and within marriage, intimacy in particular was seen as a vehicle to bring Divine blessing into the world. If the tradition has been reticent, it is because of the holiness of intimacy, not its shame.

Quite remarkably, two of the greatest *Rishonim* (medieval halachic authorities) compiled "sex manuals" for married couples that eloquently make these very points –Rabbi Avraham Ben David (*Ravad* III) in *The Holy Gate*, and Rabbi Moshe Ben Nachman (*Ramban*, although here the attribution is a little less certain) in the *Holy Letter*. (Note especially the term "Holy" that appears in both titles.) These are eye-opening, indeed revolutionary, treatments of topics rarely addressed in any sacred literature, and definitively dispel any notion that Judaism views intimacy in a negative or inferior light. Sadly, however, these works were inaccessible to those not conversant in rabbinic Hebrew, and these vital and valuable perspectives were simply lost.

We thus owe Dr. Moshe Kuhr a tremendous debt of gratitude for bringing these truths to the forefront. Dr. Kuhr, who has already made major contributions in his translations and commentaries on Maharal, has once again performed a major service in translating and annotating these two works. His translation is clear and felicitous, and his notes exhibit careful and honest scholarship. May his efforts to bring these beautiful works to the attention of the public be successful, and may their wisdom enhance the *shalom bayit* that brings the *Shechina* into the world.

With Gratitude and Admiration,

Yitzchak A. Breitowitz
Rav, Kehillas Ohr Somayach
Jerusalem, Israel

Dedicated to

Phyllis

Who has brought holiness to my life, *Baruch HaShem*,
for 63 years.

CONTENTS

שער הקדושה
The Holy Gate

רבינו אברהם בן דוד (הראב"ד)

by Ravad
(Rabbenu Avraham ben David of Posquierre)

[being the seventh chapter of the treatise
Baalei Hanefesh on Laws relating to Women]

Introduction to *The Holy Gate*

BY MOSHE KUHR

IN THE TWELFTH CENTURY, Torah flourished in Spain and Provence, notably in the realms of Halacha, Kabbala and philosophy. It happens that three sages were born around the same time, circa 1110, with the same acronym, Ravad. Ravad I, Rabbenu Avraham ibn Daud was a Spanish Talmudist, philosopher, and physician, best known for his historical work *Sefer HaKabbala*, which chronologically documents history from Adam, refuting the Karaites. Raavad II, Rabbenu Avraham Av Bet Din of Narbonne was a jurist, halachist, Kabbalist, and teacher of both Ravad III, who became his son-in-law, and Rabbenu Zerachia HaLevi, the Baal HaMor.

Ravad III, Rabbenu Avraham ben David of Posquieres, was rosh yeshiva, Talmudist and Halachist. Meiri referred to him as the "greatest of commentators" and placed him alongside Rif and Rashi. Ravad III harshly criticized Rambam's *Mishne Torah*, mainly because Rambam failed to follow the precedent of citing the sources of halachot. Rambam revered Ravad III and accepted much of his criticism. Ravad III in turn testified that *Mishne Torah* was a monumental accomplishment.

Baalei HaNefesh is Ravad III's compendium on the laws of family purity, with treatises on the menstrual cycle, immersion, and mikva construction, extensively quoted in *Tur* and *Shulchan Aruch*. The last treatise of *Baalei HaNefesh,* a halachic perspective of the intimate relationship between man and woman – husband and wife – is called *Shaar HaKedusha*, *The Holy Gate*, for Ravad III makes clear that sexual intercourse is an act of holiness. Ravad III's language is refreshing, uninhibited, and accessible. As is his way, he attributes everything he says to other sages and texts, but does not hesitate to disagree.

The modern reader may marvel at the relevance of this 900-year-old work. This is because it is but a link in a chain of Torah, from Sinai and the prophets, the rabbis of the Talmud of blessed memory, to the Rishonim. Virtually every assertion he makes is a citation from a previous source – Tanach, Talmud, Midrash, or Kabbala.

At the time that this work was written, the role and status of women differed from the mores and attitudes of today (an understatement), but Ravad shows a particular sensitivity to women. The holiness of the sex act pervades the text and the metaphor of the union of man with woman parallels *Hashem*'s Unity, *Knesset Yisrael*'s unity with *Hakadosh Baruch Hu*, *Malchut* with *Tiferet*. Much depends on the spiritual intent of the couple. Taken seriously, thoughts at the moment of union can propel the loving couple to the high reaches of holiness.

Prof. Isadore Twersky, former Chairman of Jewish Studies at Harvard University and Talner Rav wrote his Doctoral Thesis on Ravad, published by Harvard University Press as *Ravad of Posquieres* [1962]. He writes of *The Holy Gate*:

> This chapter, in many ways a first in Jewish literature – discusses, on an abstract theoretical level which nevertheless, has practical-moral implications, the ethical norms that enable one to attain purity of heart and action. It evolves a philosophy of sublime, religiously impeccable living. It outlines principles whereby plain, instinctual hedone can be elevated, endowed with purpose, and combined with spiritual motivation.

The bringing to light of such controversial material was bound to incite a response, provided by his yeshiva mate, Rabbenu Zerachia HaLevi, the Baal HaMor, who responded poetically that *The Holy Gate* was all true, but should not have been written as it could be considered a violation of a sense of *tzniut* [modesty]! His poem, *Sela Hamachloket*, is found after the translation of *The Holy Gate*.

Igeret Hakodesh – The Holy Letter, attributed to Rabbenu Moshe ben Nachman (Ramban) is a treatise on a similar theme in the form of advice to a perplexed young man about to marry. The common usage of the word "holy" in the titles attests to the sanctity of the sexual union of man and his wife.

I must express my gratitude to my dear teachers and rabbis Rav Berel Wein *z"l*, Rav Yitzchak Breitowitz, and Rav Yaakov Haber, for their guidance and encouragement. Two of my sons, Hillel and Idan helped immensely with research and early editing. Special thanks and kudos to my publisher Tzvi Mauer who worked alongside me to gently prod me to enhance the final product. And most of all to my wife Phyllis, who has been inspiring me and leading me through her *midot tovot* for sixty-three years.

Moshe David Kuhr
Kislev 5785

Chapter One

Holiness Defined

I HAVE SEEN FIT to explain the holy matters that a man needs at the time of physical intimacy in his deeds and his thoughts. Our rabbis of blessed memory said, that anyone who sanctifies himself at the time of intimacy will have sons capable to teach Torah [Shav.18b], as it says, "You shall sanctify yourselves and be holy" [*Vayikra* 11:44], followed by "to differentiate between holy and profane and between the impure and the pure" [*Vayikra* 11:47], followed by "A woman who gives seed and bears a male child" [*Vayikra* 12:2]. I wish to elaborate in this chapter on this point, for it is a matter that most people stumble upon.

First, I will explain the two types of holiness mentioned in this verse, and that which Rabbi Pinchas ben Yair says in his famous *baraita*, "purity brings about holiness" [*Yer. Shekalim* 3:3]. I will explain what purity [*tahara*] is, and what holiness [*kedusha*] is, but first I will deal with the two types of impurity [*tum'a*]; the palpable and the impalpable.

The palpable impurities are touching or carrying carcasses, creeping animals, lying or sitting in the case of *zav, zava or metzora,* seeing seminal emission, or touching the body of a dead person, or one who transgresses a sin like forbidden sexual relations, as it is written, "Do not contaminate [*titamu*] yourself with all these" [*Vayikra* 18:24], or eat forbidden food [*Vayikra* 11:43].

ראיתי לפרש בו עניני הקדושה שהאדם צריך להתקדש בשעת תשמיש במעשיו ובמחשבתו כמו שאמרו רז"ל כל המקדש עצמו בשעת תשמיש הויין לו בנים זכרים בעלי הוראה שנאמר והתקדשתם והייתם קדושים וסמיך ליה להבדיל בין הקודש ובין החול ובין הטמא ובין הטהור. וסמיך ליה אשה כי תזריע וילדה זכר. ואני רוצה להאריך בשער הזה מפני שיש תועלת באריכותו, והוא מן הענינים שרוב בני האדם נכשלים בהם. ואפרש תחלה מה הן שתי קדושות הללו הנזכרות בפסוק זה. וכן מה שאמרו בבריתא ר' פנחס בן יאיר אומר טהרה מביאה לידי קדושה, אפרש מה היא טהרה ומה היא קדושה, ומזה תדע מה הם שתי הקדושות.

ואומר תחלה כי הטומאות הם שני פנים, הטומאות הנמצאות במשוש ושלא במשוש, כגון במגע נבלות והיסטן ומגע שרצים ומשכבות ומושבות בזב וזבה ומצורע וראיית הקרי וטומאת המת, וכן העובר עברות כגון הבא על העריות והאוכל דברים האסורים, אלה הטומאות שהן במישוש, כי הבא על העריות והאוכל את האיסורין נקרא טמא כדכתיב בפרשת עריות אל תטמאו בכל אלה ובפרשת שרצים כתיב ולא תטמאו בהם ונטמתם בם.

והטומאה שהיא שלא במישוש כגון ראיית העינים ושמיעת האזנים ומבטא השפתים בדבר שאין ראוי לו לראות ולא לשמוע ולא לדבר בו, והרהור הלב בדברים שהם של איסור.

The impalpable impurities are that which the eye sees, that which the ear hears or the lips express which are improper and forbidden thoughts.

Purity [*tahara*] is also found in palpable and impalpable forms, for the various impure states can be reversed by immersion in a *mikva* or sprinkling with *chatat* water,[1] which is palpable. The impalpable impurities are reversed by separating one's self from sin, cleanliness of heart and thought and language, and avoidance of seeing and hearing the improper. All these are called "purities" as it is written, "You shall purify yourselves of all your sins before *Hashem*" [*Vayikra* 16:30] and "eyes purified from seeing evil" [*Chabakuk* 1:13], as it is written, "with clean hands and a pure heart" [*Tehilim* 24:4]. If he is careful to avoid them, he is called *tahor* [pure] and if he is not, he is called *tamei* [impure], and if he speaks unseemly words, he is called impure of lips, but if he is careful to avoid this, he is called pure of lips.

But there is a point between separating oneself from the impurities of sin and separating oneself from palpable impurities. The latter are called simply *tahor* while the former is called *tahor v'kadosh,* as it is written, "and you shall make yourselves holy and be holy" [*Vayikra14*:8]. Furthermore, the palpable impurities do not involve impurity of thought as do impurities of sin, which always have a thought component, such that he must separate from both the thought and deed of sin. If he has an improper thought, like forbidden sexuality, he must force himself to expunge it from his heart. Moreover, he must not allow himself to conclude the thought, for the concluded thought brings him to the deed and is as important as the deed, as it says, "in order that I take the house of Israel in their heart" [*Yechezkel* 14:5]. This is the second holiness the verse warns about – make yourself holy in deed and thought. As it says at the end of the verse, "for I am holy" – holy in thought and holy in deed.

גם הטהרה נמצאת במשוש ושלא במשוש, כי טהרת המגעות וההיסטות והקרי והנגעים וטומאת המת היא על ידי טבילות והזאות ושאר ענינים המפורשים במצורע, וזו היא טהרת המישוש. והטהרה שהיא שלא במישוש היא פרישת העברות והאיסורין ונקיות הלב והמחשבה והלשון ועצימת עינים ואטימת האזנים מראות ברע ומשמוע. וכל אלו הם נקראים טהורים כדכתיב מכל חטאותיכם לפני ה' תטהרו, וכתיב מכל טומאותיכם ומכל גלוליכם אטהר אתכם, וכתיב טהור עינים מראות ברע, וכתיב אוהב טהר לב חן שפתיו רעהו מלך, וכתיב נקי כפים ובר לבב. ואם הוזהר האדם מהם נקרא טהור, ואת שאינו נזהר נקרא טמא. ומי שהוא מדבר דברים שאינם ראוים לו נקרא טמא שפתים, גם הנזהר מזה נקרא טהור שפתים. נמצאת הטומאה שני פנים והטהרה שני פנים.

אלא שיש מעלה בין פרישת טומאת העברות והאיסורין לפרישת טומאות האחרות, כי הפורש מן המגעות ושאר הטומאות הדומות להם הוא הנקרא טהור לבד כדכתיב ורחץ במים וטהר, אבל הפורש מן העברות והאיסורין נקרא טהור וקדוש, טהור כאשר אמרנו, וקדוש דכתיב בפרשת עריות והתקדשתם והייתם קדושים. ולא עוד אלא כי הטומאות האחרות אין בהם טומאת מחשבה, אבל טומאת העבירות והאיסורים כמו שצריך לפרוש מגוף העברות כך צריך הוא לפרוש ממחשבותם שלא יהרהר העברה בלבו, ואם באה לו מחשבה עליהם הוא צריך לאנוס את עצמו ולהוציאה מלבו, וכ"ש שלא יתכוון לגמור אותה בלבו, לפי שהמחשבה הנגמרת היא המביאה לידי מעשה, וחשובה עליו כמעשה, ועל זו נאמר למען תפוש את בית ישראל בלבם, וזאת היא הקדושה השניה שהזהיר הכתוב עליה, והתקדשתם במעשה, והייתם קדושים במחשבה. הלא תראה מה שאמרו בסוף המקרא כי קדוש אני, כמו שאני קדוש במעשה ובמחשבה כך תהיו אתם קדושים. הא למדת שאין האדם נקרא קדוש עד שיתקדש במעשה ובמחשבה.

1. Water mixed with ashes of the red heifer.

Chapter Two

Prishut – The Fence Around the Holy

Now you understand and are aware that man cannot reach this attribute without putting aside some of that which is permissible, and contain himself within the boundaries of separation from some of what is permissible to him. For example, extending his hand below the beltline [*Shabbat* 41a] or grasping his penis while urinating, which is said to bring floods to the world.[2] Rabbi Yosi said that he never looked at his circumcision, and Rabbi Yehuda haNasi never put his hand below his belt [*Shabbat* 118b]. All these *prishot* [separations] are boundaries, to set one apart from sexual impropriety, for the evil inclination incites a person to sexual desire, and teaches him to satiate his soul and fulfill all his permissible desires to excess. As his soul hungers and does not find the desired excesses, the evil inclination subverts him to fulfill his desire with a minor transgression, then to progress to a major one, then to an even more serious transgression. It could progress to the point that he denies the One who spoke and the world came into being, believing that there is no judgment and no judge, no Garden of Eden and no Gehinnom and no future world.

Similarly, King Shlomo says, "There is an evil which is done under the sun…, for he who attaches himself to life has faith, for a living dog is better than a dead lion. For the living know they will die and the dead know nothing" [*Kohelet* 9:3–5]. Then he

ועתה תבין ותדע כי לא יוכל האדם להגיע אל המדה הזאת עד שיניח ממה שהוא מותר לו חלק מחלקיו, ויגדור את עצמו בגדר הפרישות מן הדברים המותרים לו שהם דרך ומסלול להרגל העבירה כענין שאמרו כל המכניס ידו למטה מטבורו תקצץ ידו על טבורו. וכמו שאמרו כל האוחז באמה ומשתין מים כאילו מביא מבול לעולם. וכמו שאמר ר' יוסי מעולם לא נסתכלתי במילה שלי והקשו עליו אם כן לקריוה רבינו הקדוש, אמרי רבי מילתא יתירא הואי ביה שלא הכניס ידו תחת אבנטו. וכל הפרישה הזאת היתה גדר מפני שלא תתגבר עליהם הערוה תאותה לפי שהיצר מתקוטט עם האדם ומקטרג אותו להשיאו ולהסיתו וכן הוא דרכו משיאו להשביע את נפשו ולמלא כל תאותו בכל המותר לו, ואחר אשר למדו למלא כל תאותו, ברעבון נפשו כאשר לא תמצא ידו במותר לו יסיתנו למלא תאותו מן האסור

---

2. Rabbi Dr. Natan Slifkin in *Sacred Monsters* lists five ways to deal with problematic statements of the rabbis – 1] The rabbis are always right and the conventional wisdom or science is wrong, 2] Conventional wisdom or science is right and the rabbis wrong, 3] The rabbis were speaking allegorically to teach a lesson, not to be taken literally, 4] They are both right but nature itself has undergone change, and 5] The rabbis are correct, but we do not have the intellectual tools to make sense of it. The penis and the floods story probably falls into the fifth category. Kabbalistically, the ninth sefira, *Yesod*, gathers the *shefa* and passes it to *Malchut*. If the seed is spilled, the waters of *Bina* can flow outside the proper holy channel.

says, "Go your way, eat your bread with joy… At all times your clothing shall be white, do not lack oil on your head, enjoy life with a woman you love all the days of your life. Whatever your hand finds to do, do it with your power, for there is no deed or accounting or awareness or wisdom in the Hell you are going to" [*Kohelet* 9:7–10].

The words of this wisest of men are perplexing.[3] Know that these are the words of the evil inclination, the words that subvert a person, that say, "Know you will surely die and no one in the world will save you and there is no reward, and any memory of the dead is forgotten and the love of him and the hatred of him are lost. Is it not true that a live dog is better than a dead lion? Therefore, do not lose any chance to benefit yourself in this world – go ahead and eat your bread with joy." Therefore, do not lose the benefits of this world that *Hashem* wants you to have. Now eating bread with joy and enjoying the woman you love are examples of permissible activities that may serve as minor concessions to the evil inclination. All the above subvert one with pleasures of the flesh next step is to take with force what your hand finds – this is subversion to do illicit acts like sexual perversion. All these are words of the evil inclination, who then tells him, "Know you will certainly die and no one will ever save you. Furthermore, there is no reward or punishment, so you might as well enjoy this world to the fullest."

Till here, *Kohelet* is the voice of Satan subverting him with bodily pleasure, first permissible, then forbidden. Similarly, the rabbis said that anyone who smashes a vessel in his anger[4] should be seen as an idolator, for he is given over to the evil inclination, who today says to smash a vessel and tomorrow will say worship an idol [*Shabbat* 105b]. Therefore, one must strengthen one's self and stand with his soul to do battle with his desires, so his human spiritual soul should rise above his animal soul. Desire conquers a person out of the power of the animal soul,[5] which is why the wicked, drawn after their desire, are compared to animals, as it is written, "But man does not abide honor, he is

הקל, ומן הקל אל החמור, ומן החמור אל החמור ממנו עד שאומר לו לך עבוד עבודה ותכפור במי שאמר והיה העולם שאין דין ולא דיין ולא גן עדן ולא גיהנם ולא עולם אחר.

וכן אמר החכם בספר קהלת זה רע בכל אשר נעשה תחת השמש כי מקרה אחד לכל וגם לב בני האדם מלא רע והוללות בלבבם בחייהם ואחריו אל המתים, כי מי אשר יחבר אל החיים יש בטחון וכו׳ כי החיים יודעים שימותו והמתים אינם יודעים מאומה וכו׳ גם אהבתם גם שנאתם וכו׳. ואחריה לך אכול בשמחה לחמך וכו׳. בכל עת יהיו בגדיך לבנים ושמן על ראשך אל יחסר, ראה חיים עם אישה אשר אהבת כל ימי חיי וגו׳. כל אשר תמצא ידך לעשות בכחך עשה כי אין מעשה וחשבון ודעת וחכמה בשאול אשר אתה הולך שמה.

כל אלה דברי יצה״ר הם שהוא מסית את האדם ואומר לו דע כי מות תמות ואין מי שינצל בעולם מן המיתה, ועוד שאין לו שכר והמת כבר נשכח זכרו גם אהבתו גם שנאתו כבר אבדה, והלא הכלב החי הוא טוב מן האריה המת, ועל כן לא תאבד הנאותיך בעולם הזה לך אכול וגו׳ כי כבר רצה האלהים את מעשיך וכו׳, אין לך רצון אחר ממנו אלא שתהנה מן העולם הזה לך אכול בשמחה וגו׳, בכל עת יהיו בגדיך לבנים. עד כאן הוא מסיתו בהנאת הגוף. ראה חיים עם אשה אשר אהבת וגו׳ הרי

---

3. The inclusion of Kohelet in the canon was disputed by the rabbis because of nihilistic and hedonistic statements. Shlomo considered the various fulfillments of his desires and concluded, "The sum of the matter, when all has been considered: Fear *Hashem* and keep His commandments, for that is the whole of man" [Eccl. 12:13]. Kohelet was included in the Tanach based on this verse.

4. Kohelet seems to contradict himself, saying on the one hand that everyone dies, and on the other that souls can return to their source above or fall below to Hell in pursuit of their evil desires. Ravad's answer is that we can only see the end of life in this world – the same grave for us all, but after He separates the soul from the body, the soul may ascend or descend.

5. Rabbi Sheur Zalman of Liadi, author of *Tanya*, describes two chambers of the heart, a Godly chamber on the right whose source is the Infinite Light, and an animal soul on the left, whose source is the *sitra achara*. The animal soul contains the life force and the four powers of impurity, three of which are irremediable, and the fourth, the *klipa noga*, can be rendered holy by the person.

compared to animals that perish" [*Tehilim* 49:13]. And the sage says, "Who knows the human spirit that rises to the heights and the animal spirit that descends below to earth?" [*Kohelet* 3:21].

Earlier in *Kohelet* 3, he says everyone goes to a single place, the place of his bodily origin, dust to dust.[6] Given the limited intellect of man in this world, he cannot see beyond the grave. Only *Hashem* can. The human spirit refers to the soul of the righteous which rises above, and the animal spirit refers to the soul of the wicked which is compared to the animal. The soul of the wicked lusts for the vanities of the world and its pleasures, and does not remember his ancient origins, and will return to the place of its desire. This is known, without proof, to the wise who have the capacity to think. Had *Hashem* given us a sign, even fools would know the secret of life and death.

Thus, we have learned that all souls are equal in death, all returning to their place of origin, the place they sought in their lives. The soul of the *tzaddik*, whose origin was *sechel*, and desired the place from which he came, to there he will return. The soul of the evildoer who lusts after the vanities and pleasures of this world and does not remember his origins above will return in death to the place of his lust. Had the world been created without the lusting of the evil inclination, and man would not have a desire for food or drink or sex, there would be no reason for the activities of the creatures. This would be advantageous to the sinners who would otherwise be lost in their desires and disadvantageous to the righteous who would lose their reward for resisting their temptations. The Divine Will is that the righteous must contend with their desires constantly, to direct their minds to the will of He who possesses them, and their reward is great beyond imagining, as the prophet says, "No eye has seen it beside *Hashem* Himself, for those who wait for Him" [*Yeshayahu* 64:3].

Originally, the Will of the Creator brought about the creation of His world, and created man in his uniqueness, and from him made a helper next to him, and placed upon him everlasting

זאת הסתה בהנאת הנפש ותאות היצר, ועד כאן מסיתו בדבר היתר. כל אשר תמצא ידך בכחך עשה, הרי זו הסתה בעריות ובשאר העבירות. כי אין מעשה וחשבון זהו לית דין. ודעת וחכמה לית דיין כלומר אין מי שידע במעשיך. הא למדת דרך הסתת היצר מן ההתר אל האסור ומן הקל אל החמור. וכן אמרו רבותינו כל המשבר כלי בחמתו יהיה בעיניך כעובד עבודה זרה מפני שהוא מסור ביד יצרו והיום אומר לו עשה כך ולמחר אומר עבוד עבודה זרה. ועל כן צריך האדם להתחזק ולהתגבר ולעמוד על נפשו ולהלחם בתאוותיו כדי שיהא לו מעלה בנפשו על נפש הבהמה שאין לה מעצור מכל אשר תשיג לתאותה. כי התאוה המתגברת על האדם היא מכח הנפש הצומחת והיא הבהמית, ועל כן נמשלו הרשעים הנמשכים אחר תאותם כבהמות כמו שנ׳ אדם ביקר בל ילין נמשל כבהמות נדמו, ואמר החכם מי יודע רוח בני האדם העולה היא למעלה ורוח הבהמה היורדת היא למטה לארץ, רוח בני אדם ר״ל על נפש הצדיקים שהיא עולה למעלה, ורוח הבהמה היורדת רצה לומר על נפש הרשעים שנמשלו כבהמה.

ויש מן המפרשים שאמרו כי הא העולה והא היורדת אינן מן התימה כי אם הידיעה בעבור קמצות הא העולה ודגשות יוד היורדת שהם סימני הידיעה. ואני אומר כי מלת היא תוכיח על הא התימה, והם זרות בנקוד כשאר הזרות הנמצאות במקרא. או תחסר משם מלת מי, ותכונתו להיות ומי יודע רוח בני האדם העולה מי היא למעלה ורוח הבהמה היורדת מי היא למטה לארץ, וידוע היה אצלו כי רוח הצדיק עולה למעלה במותו, ורוח הרשע יורדת שאול.

אבל אינו ענין הנכר. וענין הדברים כך הוא, כי אמר למעלה מזה הכל הולך אל מקום אחד הכל היה מן העפר והכל שב אל העפר, כלומר אין הפרש במיתה בין הצדיקים והרשעים ואף לא בין האדם והבהמה, כי כלם ימותו וישובו אל העפר ואין בכל החיים מי שיכיר מעלה בין זה לזה. ומי יודע במעלת הנפשות אם נפש הצדיק תעלה למעלה ואם תרד נפש הרשע למטה לארץ, כלומר למטה מן הארץ והוא שאול העמוק, אין בכל החיים מי שיכיר באותה המעלה כי אם הבורא לבדו. והעניין הזה

6. Man had been formed from earth. Gen. 2:7: And He formed man from the dust of the earth.

love and desire, as it is written, "He put the world in their hearts" [*Kohelet* 3:11], and commanded them, "Be fruitful and multiply" [*Bereishit* 1:28] and settle the world, as it is written, "He did not create it to be desolate; He formed it to be settled" [*Yeshayahu* 25:38]. After this commandment, he warned the man to cleave to his wife and not to someone else's wife, and various other sexual offenses. Therefore, we need to select the permissible sexual behavior from among the range of the forbidden. The Creator gave us this commandment twice, to Adam and his wife [*Bereishit* 1:28] and to the sons of Noach [*Bereishit* 9:1]. Furthermore, He warned not to diminish the husband's marital obligations, "her food, her shelter and her sexual satisfaction" [*Shemot* 21:10]. To fulfill two positive and one negative commandment carries a great reward, and to negate that reward one would be foolish.

ידוע מן החכמה אצל החכמים בעלי המחשבה, אך אין בה מופת ידוע בעניין החיים והמות כי כולם הם שווים זה לזה, ועל כן אמר ומי יודע כלומר ומי מכיר במעלתם כי אלו היה בהמעלה מופתית היו החכמים והטפשים מכירים אותה, אלא שאין בה אות ומופת בחיים ובמות.

והנה למדנו כי נפשות כלם שוות במותם שבות אל מקום תאותם והשתדלם בחייהם, כי נפש צדיק הלקוחה ממקום השכל והחזיקה בשכלה והתאוותה למקום מוצאה שמה תשוב במותו. ונפש הרשע המתאוה בהבלי העולם ובהנאותיו ולא זכרה מוצאותיה מקדם תשוב במותו אל מקום תאותה. ואילו נברא העולם בדרך שלא יצטרך האדם לתאות היצר ולא יתאוה לא למאכל ולא לשמוש כמה היתה תקנה גדולה לרשעים האובדים בתאותם והנדחים ביצרם. כי אך היה הפסד גדול בשכר הצדיקים שהם נלחמים בתאותם תמיד ושכרם מרובה עד אין חקר ותכלה, כאשר אמר הכתוב עין לא ראתה אלוהים זולתך יעשה למחכה לו.

ואחרי אשר היה רצון הבורא וברא עולמו כרצונו, וברא את האדם יחידי וממנו ברא לו עזר כנגדו, והטיל עליו אהבת עולם ותאותו כמו שאמר הכתוב גם את העולם נתן בלבם, וצוה עליהם מצות פריה ורביה כדי לישב עולמו כמו שאמר לא תוהו בראה לשבת יצרה. ואחרי המצוה ההיא הזהיר על האדם שידבק באשתו ולא באשת חברו, והזהיר כמה אזהרות וכמה עונשין על חעריות, על כן אנו צריכין לברר את המותר מתוך האיסור, וקבול השכר מתוך שלום העון. כי הבורא צוה על המצוה הזאת שתי פעמים, לאדם ולאשתו פרו ורבו, וכן בבני נח ואתם פרו ורבו שרצו בארץ ורבו בה והזהיר עוד עליה שארה כסותה ועונתה לא יגרע והמקיים שני מצות בעשה ואחד בלא תעשה שכר הרבה יש בדבר, והמפסיד את שכרו בקלקול המעשה ובגועל מחשבתו ראוי להקרא בער וסכל ופתי.

Chapter Three

The Four *Mitzvot* of Sexual Intimacy

Now, we must know and understand the proper thought that accompanies this virtuous deed, cohabitation with one's wife, and the corruptive thought that nullifies his reward. I have investigated and sought and discovered only four intentions, no more. Of the four, three are the main intents for which one receives reward, and the fourth carries less than the three. These are the four intents:

1. The intent to be fruitful and multiply, the most proper intent of all, which is the twice mentioned positive commandment.

2. The intent to fulfill the commandment to sexually gratify his wife, included in the precept "not to diminish" [*Shemot* 21:10].[7] There are times when the wife has a desire, and the husband recognizes she is trying to make him willing by adorning herself before him to make him pay attention to her. Likewise, when he is about to go on the road or returns, she has a particular desire for him. For this intent he can certainly be rewarded for fulfillment of "not denying her sexual gratification," her needs and her pleasure.

ועתה יש עלינו לדעת ולהבין אי זה היא המחשבה הנכונה באותו המעשה, ואי זו היא המחשבה המקלקלת אותו והמאבדת את שכרו והמביאה עליו רעה תחת טובה. והנה חקרתי ודרשתי במעט שכלי ומצאתי תוכן המעשה הזה על ארבע כוונות לבד, ועל החמישית לא מצאתיו. ומן הארבע כוונות מצאתי בהן שלש שהן עיקר קיבול השכר, והרביעית שכרה מועט מן השלש. והרי אני מפרש הדברים על אופניהם, הארבע כוונות אשר המעשה ההוא נכון עליהם.

הראשונה לשם פריה ורביה והיא נכונה שבכולם שהוא מקיים בה שתי מצות עשה, ומצות העונה שהוא בלא יגרע.

והשנית אע"פ שאין בה לא זה ולא זה אלא שהיא משתוקקת אליו והוא מכיר בה שהיא משתדלת ומרצה אותו ומתקשטת לפניו כדי שיתן דעתו עליה. וכן בעת צאתו לדרך שבודאי הרי היא משתוקקת אליו, גם על זו יש קבול שכר והיא מצות העונה שאמרה תורה דמיון שארה כסותה לא יגרע שהם צרכי האשה והנאותיה.

---

7. Rashi: *sh'era* is food, *k'suta* is clothing, *ona* is sexual gratification. Gur Arye: Rashi is quoting Mechilta and the Gemara [Ketubot 47b] and many *poskim* [decisors]. This position, that the Torah mandates the marital obligation of the husband to provide food, clothing and sexual gratification, is attacked by Ramban, who claims that the rabbis, and not the Torah, fixed these marital obligations. Ramban further elaborates: "*She'er* everywhere means flesh – why call it food here? Rather it means 'closeness of flesh' as in the permission granted to a cohen to defile himself to bury seven first degree relatives [*she'er*]. That flesh can imply sexual

3. The intent to "improve" the fetus, as the rabbis said, that in the last two trimesters, sexual union is good for the fetus [*Nidah* 31a], whitening and energizing it.[8]

4. The intent of fencing himself off from sin through relations with his wife.[9] He may see himself beginning to succumb to his evil inclination, his eye straying from the path of health to the path of sickness and sin. He may get a lower level of reward compared to the previous three intents for his ability to rule over his inclination and stand up to his desires and heed the words of our rabbis, "Consider three things and you will not come to do a sin – know from whence you come, where you are going, and before Whom you will give an accounting" [*Avot* 3:1]. Through this and other advice of the sages [*Shabbat* 153a] a man is able to conquer his evil inclination. Since his wife is permissible to him, he does not need to contend with his desires, but rather to satisfy them in a permissible manner and not to even think about the forbidden. He gets reward for this intention of fencing himself off from forbidden intimacy and to be saved from sin. This fourth intent may include the advice of the physicians that sexual relations are beneficial to the body, but excesses in this behavior resulting from unchecked lust can be hazardous to health.

והשלישית לתקון הולד כמו שאמרו רבותינו ז״ל שלשה חדשים הראשונים קשה לאשה וקשה לולד, אמצעיים קשה לאשה ויפה לולד, אחרונים יפה לזה ולזה שמתוך כך נמצא הולד מלובן ומזורז. וגם זו הכוונה נמשכת בכונת פריה ורביה.

והרביעית שהוא מתכוין לגדור את עצמו בה כדי שלא יתאוה לעבירה כי הוא רואה את יצרו מתגבר ומתאוה אל הדבר ההוא ואולי יצא ענינו לידי חולי מדרך הרפואות. גם בזו יש בה שכר אך לא כראשונות לפי שהיה יכול לרדות את יצרו ולעמוד נגד תאותו בהזכרת ענינים קשים המתרגשים בעולם, והויית האדם מן האפס וסופו אל ההבל, וגבורת הבורא ומכותיו הקשות אל המורדים ואל הפושעים, כענין שאמרו רבותינו הסתכל בשלושה דברים ואין אתה בא ליד עבירה דע מאין באת ולאן אתה הולך ולפני מי אתה עתיד ליתן את החשבון. וכמו שאמר החכם אם ראית צורה נאה וחמדת אותה הפוך את הצורה ותראה מה יש בתוכה. והיא כמו שאמרו רבותינו ז״ל שהיא דומה לחמת מלאה זבל ופיה מלא דם. ועם כל אלה ושאר ענינים אחרים יכול אדם לכבוש את יצרו. אעפ״כ כיון שהיא לו דבר היתר אינו צריך להלחם עם תאותו רק שיסתפק מן ההיתר כדי שלא יתן דעתו אל האסור כענין שאמרו יצר תינוק ואשה תהא שמאל דוחה וימין מקרבת. ויש לו שכר על זה כי הוא מתכוין לגדור עצמו מן העריות ולהנצל בה מן החטא. הרי אלו ארבע הכוונות הנכונות אל המעשה הזה, ואם יש בו חמישית בדברי הרופאים שהיא מועלת לגוף הרי זו נכנסה בכלל הכוונה הרביעית, כי בהתגבר היצר והרבות התאוה בא הנזק ההוא, והנגדר מזה ינצל מן הנזק ההוא.

---

closeness we know from 'and he shall cleave to his wife and they shall be one flesh' [Bereshit 2:27]. *She'er* is the skin-to-skin aspect of sexuality. He should not conduct himself as do the Persians, who have sexual relations with their clothes on! *K'sut* means proper bedding and sheets, as in 'it is his only *k'sut* – what should he sleep on?' [Shemot 22:26]. *Ona* is the time of endearment when the couple come together." But the Ramban must be in error for I [Gur Arye] cannot find it anywhere.

8. As this is not current medical wisdom, it might be a case of "change in nature" discussed in note 5.

9. Avot 1:2: Make a fence around the Torah.

There is a distinction between the first three and the fourth intention. If one intends the essential three, one has the great reward of fulfilling the commandment according to its law and for its sake, but if one intends it just for one's personal pleasure there is no reward. The fourth, default intent, to be rescued from sin, applies when he fulfills his lust and as a result, turns aside his evil inclination, is dangerously close to the loss of his reward. But if he has no desire, and provokes it by way of self-stimulation to erection to fulfill the desire of his heart for worldly pleasure, this is the way of the counsel of evil inclination. To turn away from this, **he should seek the life with the wife he loves**. As the rabbis said, a person who stimulates himself intentionally should be excluded, for he provokes the evil inclination [*Nidah* 13b]. He is compared to a satiated person who continues to overeat to the point of vomiting as some animals do.

אך יש הפרש בין הכוונה הרביעית לשלש הראשונות, אם יתכוין לעצם הכוונות שאמרנו יש לו שכר גדול כאדם המקיים המצות כהלכתם ולשמן, ואם לא יתכווין כי אם להנאת עצמו כיון שאין בה לא מצות פריה ולא תיקון ולד ולא תביעת האשה שאמרה שאינה צריכה, אין לו שכר. ואם הוא צריך לאותו דבר צריך הוא לתת שכר למעשהו ותהא כונתו להנצל בה מן החטא, ואם לא נתכוון כי אם למלאות תאותו מן הנאות העולם הנה הוא בדרך הסתת היצר ורחוק מן השכר וקרוב להפסד. אבל מי שאינו צריך לאותו דבר ואין יצרו מתגבר עליו והוא מעורר תאותו ומביא עצמו לידי קישוי ותאוה כדי להשביע יצרו ולמלא את תאות לבו מהנאות העולם ותאותיו גם אין בו אחת מן השלש דרכים הראשונים שאמרנו ודאי הוא הוא הדרך לעצת יצר הרע והסתתו שפירשנו בתחלה כדכתיב ראה חיים עם האשה אשר אהבת וכו׳, ומן ההיתר יביאנו אל האסור. ועל זה אמרו רבותינו ז״ל המקשה עצמו לדעת יהא בנידוי, ואמרינן לימא אסור, משום דקא מגרי יצר הרע בנפשיה. והעושה המעשה הזה דומה לאדם שהוא שבע ואוכל יותר מדאי ושותה יותר מדאי עד שהוא משתכר ואח״כ הוא מקיא ומתלכלך, כגון זה ודאי הוא דומה לבהמה שהיא אוכלת והולכת עד שיאחזה דם ותמות.

Chapter Four

Rabbi Natan's Ten Categories of Children

THERE ARE OTHER THOUGHTS that corrupt the deed and cause him a loss of reward, switching evil for good and harmony, and sin for good deeds worthy of reward. Rabbi Natan interprets the verse "And I will separate out from you the rebels and sinners against Me" [*Yechezkel* 20:38] to mean ten categories – children of rape, children of a despised wife, children of the excommunicated, children of exchange [he thought he was sleeping with another woman], children of a rebellious wife, children of strife, children of drunkenness, children of a wife driven out of the heart, children of a mob, and children of brazenness [*Nedarim* 20b]. Rabbi Natan also interpreted the verse "You shall not turn aside after your heart" [*Bamidbar* 15:39], one should not drink from one cup with his eyes on another cup. Ravina said that this applies even if he has two wives.

They asked Mother Shalom why her children are so beautiful, to which she answered that her husband only speaks to her at night and undresses her a handbreadth and covers her a handbreadth [many contrary interpretations] as if to cover a demon. She asked him why he did this, and he said it was in order that he not put his mind on another woman, and his children might come to illegitimacy [!?].

There is a point to the explanation of this [strange] discussion. What he "spoke to her at night" was matters related to the sexual intimacy they were about to do or to appease and stimulate

עוד יש מחשבות אחרות המקלקלות את המעשה והמפסידות אותו והמחליפות עליו רעה תחת טובה ושלום עון תחת קיבול השכר, ואע"פ שיש בה אחת מן הדרכים הראשונים והיא כאותה ששנינו בחיצונה תניא אמר ר' וברותי מכם המורדים והפושעים בי אלו בני תשע מדות בני אסנ"ת מ"ש גע"ח פירוש בני אנוסה בני שנואה בני נידוי בני תמורה בני מורדת בני מריבה בני שכרות בני גרושת הלב בני ערבוביא בני חצופה. ותניא ולא תתורו אחרי לבבכם וגו' מכאן אמר ר' נתן שלא ישתה אדם בכוס זה ויתן עיניו בכוס אחר ואמר רבינא לא נצרכה אלא לשתי נשיו.

שאלו את אימא שלום מפני מה בניך יפיפים ביותר, אמרה להם כשהוא מספר עמי אינו מספר אלא בחצי הלילה מגלה טפח ומכסה טפח ודומה כמי שכפאו שד, אמרתי לו מה טעם, אמר לי כדי שלא אתן דעתי באשה אחרת ונמצאו בני באים לידי ממזרות.

והריני מפרש את כל הענינים הללו כי יש תועלת בפירושם כי מה שאמרה שהוא מספר עמה בשעת תשמיש פי' בגמרא דדוקא במילי דתשמיש שהם צורך לאותו תשמיש. א"נ כגון שהוא לרצותה ולפתותה שאינו רשאי לבעול עד שיפייסנה, כגון זה יכול לדבר לדבר עימה ולרצותה בכל עניני רצוי. אבל אם אינו צריך לרצותה אינו רשאי לדבר בדברים אחרים חוץ מדברים של אותו תשמיש. ועוד אני אפרש כי מה שאסרו לספר בדברים אחרים לא תאמר משהתחילו במעשה בלבד, אלא אף משהוזקקו לאותו מעשה נמי

willingness, for he may not proceed without her willingness. He should not talk to her about any other matter if she is already aroused, for he should not mix in any other thoughts at the time of the deed. If he makes her willing and then enters her, this is proper behavior [*Eruvin* 100b]. When the Gemara says to converse with her first [*Chagigah* 5:2], this refers to when she needs him to ready her. The prophet says that at the time of judgment "He [*Hashem*] tells a man what his conversation is" [*Amos* 4:13] which includes even extraneous conversation between man and his wife, which is reported to him at the time of judgment [*Nedarim* 20a].

I heard a reason that I find hard to comprehend for revealing a handbreadth and covering a handbreadth – to minimize skin on skin friction so as to minimize his pleasure, for his intent is to fulfill an obligation, not to enjoy. I heard this but do not understand it.[10] I further heard an explanation that uncovering makes the act possible and quickly covering prevents increasing the duration of the act. Similarly, "entrapping a demon" puts the intimate act aside and shortens its duration.

Speaking to her words of love after midnight and not earlier is in order not to be distracted by ideas heard from people's conversations during the day or arising in the morning. Such things introduce outside thoughts during the act.

This theory must be examined, for the rabbis said the fruit of the womb[11] comes as a reward for the intimate act, resulting in male offspring [*Nidah* 71a],[12] and to shorten the act would not be beneficial. But there is no diminution in the accomplishment of the *mitzvah* here, as all hearts seek Hashem and any act in the name of heaven is good, even a short one. If a person succeeds in keeping out other thoughts and delays himself in order that his wife gives seed first, intending to accomplish the commandment, Hashem will reward him. If a man is insecure in himself and hurries the deed to save himself from evil thoughts, he also is doing *Hashem*'s commandment and will be rewarded. If he tells his wife ahead of time why he is speeding up the act, she will agree with him.

אסור, והטעם כדי שלא יתערב דעת אחרת בשעת מעשה. ולמדתי את זה ממה שאמרו בעירובין במי שהוא צריך לרצותה שמפייס ואח"כ בועל וזהו דרך ארץ, מכלל דמי שאינו צריך לרצותה אינו רשאי לספר אפילו קודם בעילה. ותו אמרינן במסכת חגיגה עליה דרב דסח ושחק ועשה צרכיו, ואוקימנא שהוא צריך לריצויי. ובאמת וברור דרב דרך ארץ היה בו ובתחלה רצה ואחר כך בעל, ואי לאו דהוה צריך לרצוי הוה מקשי ליה מבריתא על שהיה מספר בשעת תשמיש, הא למדת שאף משהוזקקו לתשמיש אסור לספר חוץ מדברי תשמיש לבד, ואם סיפר מה עונשו עליו הכתוב אומר מגיד לאדם מה שיחו אפילו שיחה יתירה שבין איש לאשתו מגידין לו בשעת הדין. ובעולם הזה מה עונשו, כך אמרו רבותינו חרשין מפני מה הויין מפני שמספרין בשעת תשמיש ומאי ניהו במילי אחרנייתא.

ומה שהיה מגלה טפח ומכסה טפח, שמעתי בפירושו שלא היה ממרק כל האבר בשעת תשמיש כדי למעט הנאתו ממנה. ודומה כמי שכפאו שד, אדם שהוא עושה הדבר מאונס שאין מתכוין להנאתו כך שמעתי, ולא נתברר אצלי כי הוא נתן טעם למעשה הזה כדי שלא יתן דעתו על אשה אחרת, ואין הטעם דומה למעשה, כי היה לו לומר מפני שאיני

---

10. The marital sexual act is fulfillment of *Hashem*'s will, a Torah commandment, Divine service. Perhaps Ravad sees inhibiting enjoyment as a violation of "Serve *Hashem* with rejoicing" [*Tehilim* 100:2].

11. Perhaps this refers to lengthening the act so as to allow her to first "give seed," i.e., to climax before him. "If a woman gives seed [first], she will give birth to a male" [*Vayikra* 19:1].

12. Bereishit 46:15: These are the **sons of Leah** which she bore Yaakov in Padam Aram, and Dina, **his daughter.** Rashi: Males depend on mothers and females on fathers for if he sows first, she will bear a daughter. Gur Arye cites Rav's erroneous opinion that the upper one, the second to sow, conquers the lower one, the first to sow. This is not the way of the world *Hashem* saw fit to create. The male is attracted to the female and combines with her to achieve *shelemut* that he had before the original male/female was split, and vice versa. Her sowing first imparts her effort and her affinity to the ovum, and her attraction to the male extends not only to her mate but to her offspring as well. If he sows first, the converse applies. Each participant in the creative act strives for *hashlama* [harmonious completion] and the *hashlama* of each sex is the opposite sex.

I heard another reason why the husband of Mother Shalom "uncovered a handbreadth and covered a handbreadth" – out of modesty, she wore a type of belt which she uncovered at the time of intimate relations and covered herself with it afterward. She uncovered herself piecemeal for she feared the aforementioned demon would distract her husband. The intimacy was done in fear, for she felt she was in the presence of a demon who could disrupt her husband's thoughts. Though there was a matter of modesty, the main point was to keep him from having extraneous thoughts. The Jerusalem Talmud brings a similar example of Rabbi Yosi bar Tachlifa, who consummated his levirate marriage five times through a sheet [*Yevamot* 2:1]. This was in order that his intent was purely for the sake of the commandment.

The ten types of offspring quoted above fit this model. We learn [*Kala* 100b] that children with congenital defects result when he wants and she refuses, but he proceeds to enter her anyway. Rabbi Yehoshua says it is because she says during the act, "I am being raped." Anyone who forces his wife to do this "*mitzvah*" is called evil [*Eruvin* 100b], as it is written, "for the soul to be without *daat* [awareness, knowledge] is not good" [*Mishlei* 19:2]. Rape is forbidden with one's wife, but if he has the urge he must appease and seduce her first.

Children of a hated wife, even if the husband does not intend to divorce her, fall into the category of products of a forbidden act with a permitted woman. This is a forbidden intimacy [*b'ilat znut*], not marital intimacy. When the Torah calls Leah "hated," it is only in relation to Rachel, for whom Yaakov had an extra measure of love, but he still wanted and needed Leah.

Children of *niduy* [impurity] refers to the offspring of a menstruant, even though there is no *mamzerut* that results.

In the case of children of exchange [*temura*], he intended to do a forbidden act but later discovered the act was with his wife. Even if he had two wives, both permitted to him, and was intimate with one thinking he was with the other. Some ask on the latter case that if so, Reuven would have been a child of

רוצה להנות מן העולם ואיני עושה אלא לשם המצוה בלבד. ושמעתי עוד בפירושו כי מגלה טפח ומכסה טפח שבאשה קאמר, כלומר עכשיו מגלה אותו לצורך התשמיש, ועכשיו מכסה אותה, לומר שלא היה מאריך באותו מעשה. ודומה כמי שכפאו שד, פי' דומה כמי שהבעיתו שד ונבעת והניח את המעשה, כל כך היה מקצר את התשמיש.

ועתה לזה הפירוש יבוא הטעם לכל המעשה, כי מה שלא היה מספר עמה אלא בחצי הלילה גם הוא מאותו הטעם כדי שלא יזכור קול האנשים והנשים ששמע ביום ולא ישמע קול המשכימים בבקר. וגם קוצר המעשה הזה הוא כדי שלא תכנס שום מחשבה בתוך המעשה. אלא שיש לדקדק על זה הפירוש א"כ לא היה משהה עצמו על הבטן, וכבר אמרו רבותינו שכר פרי הבטן בשכר שמשהים עצמן על הבטן הוויין להם בנים זכרים. וזו אינה קושיא, כי כל לבבות דורש ה' וכל המעשים שהם לשם שמים טובים הם. ומי שאומד את עצמו שיוכל לעשות כך ולא תכנס עליו מחשבה אחרת, והוא משהא עצמו כדי שתהנה האשה מן המעשה ותזריע תחילה מתכוין לעשות מצוה ועושה אותה, והקב"ה נותן לו שכרו בבנים זכרים. ומי שאינו בטוח בעצמו בכך וממהר את המעשה כדי להנצל מן החטא גם הוא עושה מצוה והקב"ה משלם שכרו בבנים יפיפים, וגם הוא כבר הודיע אותה את הטעם והיתה דעתה נסכמת עמו על כך.

עוד שמעתי בפירושו כי מגלה טפח ומכסה טפח משום צניעות הוא ועל הסינר שהיא חוגרת קאמר שאף בשעת התשמיש היה מצריכה לחגרו ומגלה טפח שבה מאותו הסינר בשעת תשמיש ומכסה אותה בו אחר תשמיש ודומה כמי שכפאו שד שהיה עושה את המעשה ביראה כאדם שהוא נבעת מן השד. וכל זה כדי שלא תכנס עליו שום מחשבה אחרת. ואעפ"י שיש בענין הזה ענין צניעות עיקר כונתו לכך היתה, ודוגמת המעשה הזה אמרו בגמ' דבני מערבא ב' יוסי בר חלפתא שכנס יבמתו חמש בעילות בעל ודרך סדין בעל. ואותו הענין לא היה אלא כדי שלא תהא כונתו אלא לשם מצוה בלבד.

ובני עשר מדות שאמרנו כך הוא פירושם, בני אנוסה אין אתה צריך לומר שאנס את האשה והוליד ממנה בן אלא אף מי שאנס את אשתו בתשמיש. וכן שנינו במסכת כלה מפני מה הווין לו לאדם בנים בעלי מומין מפני שהוא תובעה ואינה נתבעת לו פי' שאינה מתרצה לו

exchange, for when he was conceived, Yaakov thought he was with Rachel when it was really Leah. However, the Torah had not been given, and anyway, we do not know if she conceived that night. Besides, the error was unintended and would not make him an intentional sinner. Since his act was unintentional and he thought she was Rachel, he did no sin and Reuven was not a *ben temura.* Additionally, the Torah had not yet been given and the details of *mitzvot* did not apply.

Children of the rebellious wife, who stated she did not want him, but he had relations with her anyway and she conceived, even if she consented, she is considered like a prostitute. A different version has it that this applies to children of strife.

Children of strife, whose parents fight with each other day and night – their marital intimacy is considered illicit [*znut*], for it does not come out of love.

Children of drunkenness who are conceived while he or she is inebriated and copulated without loving intent. Scripture likens their act to *znut,* as it is written, "Licentiousness, wine and new wine seize the heart [*Hoshea* 4:11].

Children of divorce of the heart are conceived after the father intended and concluded in his mind to divorce his wife, but had relations with her nevertheless.

Children of *irbuvia* [confusion, mixture] result from relations in which the husband was thinking of another woman during the act, even his other wife, as we explained earlier.

Children of a brazen wife who verbally demanded intimacy, she is considered as a *zona* [forbidden woman, harlot] to whom her husband may not remain married [?]. But if she uses words of *ritzui* [acceptance] and adorns herself in front of him so that he pays attention to her and comes to want her, the sages praise her. Leah did this on the night Yisachar was conceived, about whom is written, "And the sons of Yisachar, who knew and understood the calendar [*Divrei Hayamim I* 12:32].

How, then, is Leah our mother called *senua,* yet her offspring are not called *bnai senua*? *Hashem* calls her *senua* [*Bereishit* 29:31]

ואעפ"כ הוא נזקק לה, ר' יהושע אומר מפני שאומרת לו בשעת תשמיש אנוסה אני, ואיכא בינייהו רוצה ואינה רוצה. וכן אמרו במסכת עירובין כל הכופה את אשתו לדבר מצוה נקרא רע שנא' גם בלא דעת נפש לא טוב. נמצא כי האונס אסור אף באשתו אלא אם צריך הוא לאותו מעשה יפיים ואח"כ יבעול.

בני שנואה כמשמעה ואע"פ שאין בדעתו לגרשה, והטעם מפני שהיא כמו בעילת זנות ואינה כבעילת אישות. בני נידוי פי' בני נדה, ואע"פי שאין ממזר מן הנדה.

בני תמורה שהיה מתכוין לערוה ונזדמנה לו אשתו. וי"מ אפילו בשתי נשיו שהוא מתכוין לזו ונזדמנה לו האחרת והוא סבור כי היא חברתה. ויש ששואלין לזה הפירוש א"כ יש מן השבטים שהן בני תמורה שהרי יעקב אבינו ע"ה נתכוין לרחל ונזדמנה לו לאה, יש לומר שעדיין לא נתנה תורה ולא נאסרו בדקדוקי מצות. אי נמי אפשר שלא נתעברה בלילה ההוא. אלא אי קשיא הא קשיא, מאחר שהוא שוגג והוא סבור שהיא היא המתכוין אליה למה נקרא מורד ופושע, אלא מחוורתא כלישנא קמא.

בני מורדת דאמרה ליה לא בעינא לך ואעפ"כ הוא משמש עמה הרי היא אצלו כמו זונה ואפילו מדעתה.

והנוסחא האחרת בני מריבה, שהם מתקוטטים יומם ולילה הביאה ההיא אינה אלא זנות שאינה באה מתוך אהבה.

בני שכרות, שהוא שכור או שהיא שכורה ואין בהם כוונת אהבה והרי הסמיכם הכתוב זנות יין ותירוש יקח לב.

בני גרושת הלב, שבלבו לגרשה וגמר בדעתו לעשות כך ואח"כ הוא בא עליה.

בני ערבוביא, כאשר פירשנו למעלה שהוא משמש עם אשתו ונותן דעתו באשה אחרת ואפילו שתיהן נשיו.

בני חצופה, שהיא תובעת התשמיש בפיה הרי היא כזונה ואסור לקיימה.

אבל מי שאשתו מרצה אותו בדברי ריצוי ומתקשטת לפניו כדי שיתן דעתו עליה ויזדקק לה, על זו ארז"ל שיוצאין ממנה בנים זכרים ונבונים. כלאה שעשתה כן ליעקב ויצא ממנה יששכר שנאמר בו ומבני יששכר יודעי בינה לעתים.

as she calls herself [*Bereishit* 29:33] but this was only relative to Rachel, Yaakov's true love. But Yaakov our father needed and loved her and she was not *senua.*

All of these ten attributes, which affect the state of mind of the couple at the time of conception, inhibit the successful production of offspring or render defective the resultant offspring. Although the union of such couples is required to fulfill "be fruitful and multiply," if she conceives as he is thinking about another woman, or she was raped, or she had one of the ten attributes, there is a defect in the resultant offspring as well as a defect in him, as he is called a rebel and a sinner.

There are other matters that defect the deed and corrupt him and cause him to lose the reward, as the Gemara explains Rabbi Yochanan ben Dahavai said four things that the serving angels tell me: What causes lameness? They turn over their table. This means they copulate the way animals do. What causes blindness? They gaze intently at nakedness, or as some say they look at that place when they want to have sexual relations, even if he conducts himself with modesty when he does the act. If he does the act by day, he should cover with his shawl, and if by night he should put out the candle. What is worse is to gaze at the place of her nakedness at a time other than relations,[13] as this is wanton conduct that incites the evil inclination. What causes deafness? Kissing that place. What causes mutism? Talking during intercourse [?] The last is because he will put his mind on another woman. Alternatively, performing intercourse without intent to fulfill the commandment, is almost debauchery [*Nedarim* 20a].

Rabbi Yochanan, the chief decisor and leader of that generation, ruled that *halacha* is not like ben Dahavai, but **anything a married couple wish to do with one another, they may do.** It appears to me [Ravad] that he meant posterior intercourse [upending the table]. A woman came before Rav and told him she set the table for her husband and he turned it [me] over. He answered her, "So what is the difference?" which

בני שנואה, היא שאמרו ששונאה ומתרחקת בשעת תשמיש שהרי לאה אמנו היתה שנואה מפני רחל ואעפ"כ היה יעקב אבינו נזקק לה, מיהו בשעת תשמיש מיהא רצויה היתה לפניו. עוד יש לומר שהיא קראה עצמה שנואה על שלא היה אוהב אותה אהבה יתרה כמו אהבת רחל ולא היה שונאה.

וכל אלו בני עשר מדות שאמרנו אפילו יהיו צריכים לפריה ורביה שאין אשתו מעוברת והוא צריך שתתעבר ותלד, ואם תלד ומחשבתו על אשה אחרת, או שהיתה אנוסה בשעת תשמיש, או שהיו בה אחת מכל המידות האלו שזכרנו פוגם את הולד ופוגם את עצמו שהוא נקרא מורד ופושע.

עוד יש ענינים אחרים שהם פוגמין את המעשה ומקלקלין אותו ומפסידין את שכרו, והם מה שפירשו בנדרים א"ר יוחנן בן דהבאי ארבעה דברים סחו לי מלאכי השרת, חגרים מפני מה הויין, מפני שהופכים את שולחנם, פירוש נוהגין כמו מעשה בהמה. סומין מפני מה הויין, מפני שמסתכלין בערוה. וי"מ שמסתכלין בשעה שהוא רוצה לשמש, ואע"פ שבשעת המעשה הוא מצניע עצמו. ואם שמש ביום מאפיל בטליתו. ואם בלילה מכבה את הנר, כיון שעשה כן סמוך לתשמיש המטה ונהג בה מנהג הפקר. וכ"ש אם מסתכלים שם שלא בשעת תשמיש שהוא מנהג הפקר והוא מגרה היצר בעצמו כאשר פרשנו בשער הפרישה. ואלמין מפני מה הויין, מפני שנושקין באותו מקום. חרשים מפני מה הויין, מפני שמספרין בשעת תשמיש. הראשונות מפני שנהגו בה מנהג הפקר, והרביעית מפני שנותן דעתו באשה אחרת, א"נ מפני שעושה המעשה כעין זנות שאין מתכוין לו ועושה.

ומה שאמר רבי יוחנן אין הלכה כר' יוחנן בן דהבאי אלא כל מה שאדם רוצה לעשות באשתו עושה משל לדג הבא מן הצייד וכו', דמשמע שמותר לעשות כן לכתחלה, נ"ל שאינו אלא על הפיכת השולחן בלבד כדאיתא בשמעתא דההיא דאתיא לקמיה דרב אמרה לו ר' שלחן ערכתי לפניו והפכו, אמר לה מי שנא מביניתא, דמשמע נמי

---

13. Think pornography.

meant that posterior is permissible. This may not apply to other deviations.

We stated above that speaking "other things" during intercourse is forbidden unless they enhance the process, or he needs to make her willing. The rabbis said that when he is judged, he is told every conversation he ever had, even the extra [unnecessary conversations] at the time of intimacy [*Chagigah* 5b]. If he gazes at that place during intercourse, he transgresses "and walk modestly with your God" [*Micha* 6:8].[14] And it is written, "your shame shall be upon your face" [*Shemot* 20:20] – one who is embarrassed does not sin. Even worse is to kiss [that place], which includes all these citations. Additionally, he transgresses "You shall not abominate your souls" [*Makot* 16b]. Rabbi Kahana passed an unclean locust across his lips and Rav told him he transgressed – ever more so this. Upending the table is permissible only when she wants it along with him, but if she does not it would be sinful for him.

As the rabbis said, the verse "that the soul without knowledge is not good, and he who hastens his feet sins" [*Mishlei* 19:2] refers to one who copulates repetitively. How do we reconcile this with the Gemara that states that he who wants male offspring should copulate repetitively [*Eruvin* 100b]? The answer is it depends on whether or not he had the intent to have male offspring. If he had no such intent, it would be sinful. If he upends the table [posterior intercourse] without her consent, this is certainly sinful. There is an opinion that if she desires to have relations with her husband but he insists on upending the table, it is permissible, as opposed to repetitive without consent, which is debauched copulation. The proof of this is Rabi's permitting upending the table when she did not want it. I [Ravad] say this is no proof, for they both may have wanted it, and she may have wanted to know the *halacha* after the fact. The overriding principle is that **nothing is permissible without her desiring it.** We learn in Tractate Kala that if she is on top, this is brazen, and if they copulate as one [?], this is a perverse way.

מהכא דהפיכת שולחן אינו אסור, דוקא על הפיכת השולחן לבד אבל על האחרות אע"פ שאין נדון עליה דין חמור מ"מ אסור.

יש בהן כאשר אמרנו למעלה שאסור לאדם לדבר בדברים אחרים בשעת תשמיש אלא א"כ הם צרכי תשמיש או שהוא צריך לרצותה. ובמס' חגיגה אמרו מגיד לאדם מה שיחו אפילו שיחה יתירה שבין איש לאשתו בשעת תשמיש מגידין לו. וכן המסתכל בשעת תשמיש באתו מקום עובר משום והצנע לכת עם אלהיך.

ומעביר את הבושה מעל פניו. וכתיב בעבור תהיה יראתו על פניכם שכל המתבייש אינו חוטא. וכ"ש הנושק שיש בו כל אלה, ועוד שעוברין משום בל תשקצו את נפשותיכם. כאשר אמרו ז"ל מאן דשתי בקרנא דאומנא עבר משום בל תשקצו. ורב כהנא דהוה מעבר שושיבה על פומיה ואמר ליה רב שקליה דלא לימרו מיכל קא אכיל וקא עבר משום בל תשקצו, וכ"ש הך. והפיכת השולחן עצמו שהתירו אומר אני דוקא כשאינה כבודה עליו והיא מתרצית עמו לדעתה על ידי ריצוי, אבל אם הוא כופה בהפיכה ודאי אינו ניצל מן החטא ועליו נאמר גם בלא דעת נפש לא טוב.

שהרי אמרו ז"ל ואץ ברגלים חוטא זה הבועל ושונה, והקשו והא אמרינן הרוצה שיהיו לו בנים זכרים יבעול וישנה ותירצו לא קשיא כאן לדעת כאן שלא לדעת. הנה זה שבועל ושונה וכוונתו לשם בנים זכרים, וכשהוא עושה שלא לדעתה נקרא חוטא, וכל מי שהוא הופך את שולחנו שלא מדעתה כ"ש שהוא חוטא. ויש מי שאומר שמי שהופך שולחנו כיון שהיא מרוצה לתשמיש המטה אע"פ שהיא מוכרחת בהפיכה מותר, משא"כ בבועל ושונה שלא מדעתה שכל הבעילה על כרחה היא ואסור מפני שהוא בעילת זנות, והראיה על זה כי האשה שבאה לפני רבי ואמרה לו וכו' פשוטו של דבר דומה שלא היו הן רוצות ואעפ"כ התיר, ואני אומר שאין ראיה מזה, שאפשר שנתרצו להן על ידי ריצוי אלא שבאת לדרוש אם היה איסור בדבר אם לאו. וכלשון הראשון נ"ל דאסור לעשות בה שום דבר שלא מדעתה עד שיפייסנה ותתרצה. (ושנינו במסכת כלה הוא למטה והיא למעלה זו היא דרך עזות, שמשו שניהם כאחת זו היא דרך עקש.)

---

14. This may be a subtle reference to *Hashem*'s participation along with the couple in the act.

Chapter Five

Keep Her Satisfied, But Don't Let Her Dominate

The rabbis have said that the evil inclination of a child or a woman should be resisted by the left hand and brought close by the right hand [*Sotah* 47a]. Since the rabbis put man's *halachic* requirement to sexually satisfy his wife [*ona*] according to his ability and satisfaction, why should his pushing her aside be stronger than his drawing her close? This question is asked out of ignorance. First, let us define the inclination of child and woman before addressing the problem. Some say a woman's inclination is sexual. Some say it is for what he provides for her – food, drink, clothing, and jewelry, and should be given in such a way as to not get her used to completely fulfilling all her desires, making onerous the burden of supporting her. He should hold a little back, lest she dominate him by getting all she wants, for there is no bad illness worse than having a wife who dominates him.

Both solutions – her *yetzer* meaning inclination for sex[15] or her inclination for worldly desires like food and jewelry – are correct, and knowledge and wisdom can be learned from them. Fulfillment of the sex act requires some restraint, holding back with the left hand. However, the right hand should bring her close so that he satisfies his hunger and thirst and sees his soul in a state of goodness. Fulfilling one's permissible desires is a good thing, as the rabbis said that in the future, a man will have to stand in judgment for what his eyes beheld even if he

ואם ישאל השואל על מה שאמרו ז"ל יצר תינוק ואשה תהא שמאל דוחה וימין מקרבת, כיון שנתנו חכמים עונה לכל איש ואיש כפי כוחו וכפי תענוגו, כמפורש בכתבות, מה תהיה עוד דחיית השמאל והקרבת הימין, נשיב ונאמר כי מבלי דעת תוכן הענין נשאלה שאלה זו. ועתה נפרש תחלה מה הן יצר תינוק ואשה, כי יש תועלת בפתרון הענין, ואחר נשיב תשובת השאלה. יצר ואשה אמרו בפתרונם שני פנים, יש מי שאומר יצר הוא התשמיש, ואשה הוא שאר עסקי האשה כגון מאכליה ומשתיה ומלבושיה ותכשיטיה שלא ירגילנה למלא כל רצונה, אך יגער בה פעם ופעמים פן תכביד עולה עליו, גם תועיל גערתו של תתגבר עליו, כי אין רעה חולה מרעת האשה כאשר תמשול על בעלה.

ויש מי שאומר כי האשה היא התשמיש, והיצר הוא שאר תאות העולם, שיעמוד האדם כנגדן ולא ימלא נפשו מהן, וזו היא דחיית השמאל. אך תהא הימין מקרבת שיאכל לרעבו וישתה לצמאו ויראה את נפשו טוב בעמלו ולא יתענה כדי לצער את עצמו כמו שאמרו במקום אחר על המצער עצמו מן היין שנקרא חוטא וכ"ש המצער את עצמו מכל דבר. ועוד אמרו בירושלמי עתיד אדם ליתן דין וחשבון

---

15. Perhaps this means its benefits, like closeness, children, reassurance of his love, pleasing her man. It could be that some women are lustful.

did not partake of it [*Yerushalmi Kiddushin* 4:12].[16] These two interpretations, *yetzer* and worldly desires, are both correct, and one can learn knowledge and wisdom from them, for conjugal relations require the restraint of the left hand.

על כל מה שראו עיניו ולא אכל ממנו, ר"א היה מצמת פריטין בכיסיה וזבין בהו מכל מין חדא זימנא בשתא. הנה שני הפתרונים האלה נאמרו עליהן והם נכונים, ויש ללמוד מהן דעת וחכמה, ומשניהם נלמוד כי התשמיש צריך שיהא בו דחוי השמאל.

16. Perhaps this might apply to intercourse, a warning for him not to gaze at that place as he embraces her with his right arm.

Chapter Six

King David's Problem

The Gemara states that man has a small organ whose satisfaction is hunger and whose hunger satisfies[17] [*Sukkah* 52b; *Sanhedrin* 107a].[18] This refers to David, who slept by day instead of night, which caused him to stumble with Batsheva,[19] so that when he saw her bathing on her roof at night, he lusted for her [Rashi, Sanhedrin 107a].[20]

17. Rashi, *Sukkah* 52b: When it becomes sexually satiated, his body can have unfulfilled lust. Tosafot: Rabbi Yehuda in *Sanhedrin* says that [permissible] sexual excesses by day and by night causes illicit sexuality, as occurred with David.

18. *Sanhedrin* 107a: Rabbi Yehuda said in Rav's name: A person should not ask to be tested as David, King of Israel did, and he stumbled. He said, "Master of the Universe, why do they say, 'God of Avraham, God of Yitzchak, and God of Yaakov' and they do not say God of David?" *Hashem* answered, "They were tested, you were not tested." David said, "Master of the Universe, try and test me" as it is written, "Try me and test me" [Ps. 26:2:]. That very night David arose from his bed and the Batsheva story transpired [Sam. 11:11]. Rav Yehuda said he changed his routine to sleep with his women by day and stay up at night. The *halacha* was hidden from him that there is a small organ in a man which when satiated is hungry and when hungry is satisfied. Rashi says here that he sexually satiated himself by day in order not to think about women. Instead, his excesses inflamed him, and he sinned that night.

וכן אמרו במקום אחר אבר אחד יש בו באדם משביעו רעב מרעיבו שבע, והזכירו הדבר על ענין דוד שהפך משכבו של לילה למשכבו של יום ונכשל במעשה בת שבע, כי לפי שהשביע יצרו מאותו דבר התאוה אליה.

---

19. *Avodah Zara* 4b: Rabbi Yochanan said in the name of Rashbi: David was not fitting for this deed, but it was the decree of the Almighty King in order to teach sinners the opportunity to repent. David was a great and righteous individual and his sin was most egregious, yet he could repent and *Hashem* accepted his *teshuva*. See Maharal's *Netiv Hateshuva*, Ch.4.

20. *Shabbat* 56a: Rabbi Shmuel bar Nachmani said in the name of Rabbi Yonatan: Anyone who says David sinned is mistaken, as it says, "David was wise in all his ways, and *Hashem* was with him" [I Sam. 18:14]. Is it possible he sinned, yet *Hashem* was with him? How, then can I explain, "Why did you shame the word of God to do the evil [II Sam. 12:9]? He wanted to do it but he did not do it. Rav said, "My teacher, you upended the story and explained it to David's merit!" Rabi said that all the evil deeds in the Torah, it says *asa*, "did," but here it says "*laasot*," to do.

Chapter Seven

How is *Ona* Measured?

Now, let us return to the question and say that the sages assigned time measures for *ona* according to a man's potential. For example, are *tayalim,* strollers, unemployed men who are always available to their wives. It is possible that these are the men that have occasion to push them away with their left hand to establish dominance. She might assent to being pushed to avoid his passion from overcoming him in the fulfillment of his desire. But the *ona* prescribed for Torah scholars, weekly on Shabbat, certainly precludes ever pushing her away. The rabbi said, "which gives its fruit in its time" [*Tehilim* 1:3] means one Shabbat eve to the next [*Ketuvot* 62b]. Ever more so, the camel driver and the sailor would not push her away. The designated minimal time intervals [*onot*] are to guarantee the woman sufficient sexual satisfaction, and a man is not permitted to lengthen the interval without her permission. **If he needs more and she is agreeable they may be intimate anytime.**

He should balance his right arm embrace, with the restraint of the left, signifying the rabbis' admonition to not completely fulfill his ardor. The sages established the *onot* arbitrarily, estimating her response to his enticement which is based on his strength and pleasure.[21] However, should he see that she wants his sexual attention and needs it and makes an effort to signal him, for example, by bejeweling herself in front of him,

ועתה נשיב תשובת השאלה ונאמר כי אמת הוא הדבר שנתנו חכמים מדת העונות לכל אחד ואחד כפי כחו, והאחד מהן הטיילים שהם בכל יום. ואפשר כי עליהן נאמר שתהא השמאל דוחה למעט מהם מרשות אשתו ומדעתה כדי שלא יתגבר עליו יצרו במלאת תאותו. אבל מעונת תלמידי חכמים ודאי שאין למעט שהרי אמרו רבותינו ז"ל אשר פריו יתן בעתו מערב שבת לערב שבת. וכל שכן מהעונות האחרות של גמלים וספנים. עוד נאמר כי העונות שנתנו חכמים למלא תשוקת האשה הן שאינו רשאי למעט מהם אלא מדעתה, ואם יצטרך אל המעשה ההוא הרשות בידו להוסיף.

כי היא מן הרביעית מן הכונות שאמרנו להנצל בו מן העבירה, ועל דרך ההוא הזהירוהו שיעמוד כנגד יצרו ולא ימלא כל תאותו בדחיית השמאל, ותהא בו הקרבת הימין כדי שלא תבטל עונתו, כי שמא מתוך הכניעו את יצרו והלחמו עמו תבטל מצותו. עוד נאמר כי העונות שנתנו חכמים על דרך הסתם קבעו אותם, כי אמדו דעת האשה שהיא מתפייסת מבעלה בכך לפי מה שהוא כוחו ותענוגו, אבל אם יראה שהיא מבקשת אותו המעשה והיא צריכה לכך בהשתדלותה עמו ובהתקשטה לפניו הרי הוא חייב לשמחה בדבר

21. This is the rare occasion in this treatise that Ravad mentions the man's pleasure. It is clear that the primary focus of *ona* is the woman's sexual satisfaction. This might be a textual corruption.

he is obliged to make her happy by performing this *mitzvah.* Rava said a man is obligated to make his wife happy with this commandment even beyond the appointed time of *ona*, or even if she is pregnant[22] [*Pesachim* 72b]. Rabbi Yehoshua ben Levi said anyone who knows his wife, fears sin and fails to satisfy her, is called a sinner, as it is said, "And you will know that your tent is peace, and you shall visit your home and miss nothing" [Job 5:24] [*Yevamot* 62b]. Not just the Torah *mitzvah* of *ona,* as it is written, "Food, clothing, and *ona* he shall not diminish" [*Shemot* 21:10], but even other times when she needs intimacy, he should not deny her [*Yevamot* 62b]. Additionally, a man must make time to unite with his wife at a time when he is about to travel, even if she is in a state of rabbinical *veset* [separation]. Why is this permissible? The rabbis do not issue decrees that violate Torah commandments.[23]

מצוה כאשר אמרו בפסחים אמר רבא חייב אדם לשמח את אשתו בדבר מצוה אפילו שלא בשעת עונתה ואפי' היא מעוברת וכשהיא צריכה לאותו מעשה קאמר. וא"ר יהושע בן לוי כל היודע באשתו שהיא יראת חטא ואינו פוקדה נקרא חוטא שנא' וידעת כי שלום אהלך ופקדת נוך ולא תחטא, ואי בשעת עונתה דאורייתא הוא דכתיב שארה כסותה ועונתה לא יגרע, אלא לאו אפילו שלא בשעת עונתה וכשהיא צריכה לאותו מעשה. ועוד אמרו חייב אדם לפקוד את אשתו בשעה שהוא יוצא לדרך, ואמרינן התם אפילו בשעת וסתה, מאי טעמא כיון דוסתות דרבנן במקום מצוה לא גזור.

---

22. Or postmenopausal.

23. Ravad seems to be emphasizing the importance of the positive Torah [*d'araita*] *mitzvat ona* in the situation of the man departing on a long trip. *Veset* is the separation associated with the woman's menses. *Veset d'oraita* occurs as long as she is bleeding; *Veset d'rabanan* is a stringency added by the rabbis at the request of the women that the separation continues seven clean days. Ravad seems to say this *ona* trumps *veset d'rabanan*. This is not to be taken as *halacha* and any questions should be brought to an authoritative rav.

Chapter Eight

What is the Ideal Conduct for Man?

He should do what heaven desires and what his wife desires. What does heaven desire? He should spread about his money to the poor, as it says, "He dispersed widely to the poor – his righteousness endures forever" [*Tehilim* 112:9]. What does his wife desire? Rabbi Eliezer says that he should seduce her at the time they unite. Rabbi Yehoshua says he should cause her to rejoice in the *mitzvah* of their uniting. Whenever he desires her, **he is obligated to do what she desires and to make her happy.**

This is why the rabbis warn us that his left should push and his right embrace, lest she draw him to the vanities of the world. So, he needs to limit his desire and suppress his inclination by pushing with the left not to be drawn into the forbidden and be punished.

The rabbis saw that there were the totally righteous who limited themselves in various ways – avoiding nice clothing like Rabbi Yehuda bar Ilai, or separating from his wife after achieving being fruitful. Each one limited himself according to what he recognized to be his nature and saw how to fix it.

They said of the *yetzer* that Avraham perfected his people and it is said of him, "When a man's ways please *Hashem*, he makes even his enemies be at peace with him" [*Mishlei* 16:7] [*Yerushalmi Bereishit* 9:5]. David made war with the *yetzer* and

ועוד במסכת כלה מה יעשה אדם ויהיו לו בנים זכרים יעשה חפצי שמים וחפצי אשתו, אלו הן חפצי שמים יפזר מעותיו לעניים שנא' פזר נתן לאביונים, ואלו הן חפצי אשתו ר' אליעזר אומר יפתנה בשעת תשמיש, ר' יהושע אומר ישמחנה בדבר מצוה. ואחרי שראינו כל אלה שהאדם חייב לעשות חפצי אשתו ולשמחה במצוה זו בכל עת שהיא צריכה לה.

על כן הזהירונו שתהא שמאל דוחה וימין מקרבת פן תסיתנו לעבור על המידה ותמשכהו אחריה אל הבלי העולם ויאבד בעבורה. וע"כ צריך אדם לשבר תאותו ולהכניע את יצרו בדחיית השמאל כדי שלא יבא לידי איסור ויגיע לידי עונש.

ראינו לרבותינו ז"ל שהיו חסידים גמורים והיו גודרים את עצמם בכמה גדרים, והיה מהן מי שלא היה רוצה להינות במלבושים נאים כגון ר"י בר אלעאי, והיה מהם מי שפירש מאשתו אחר שקיים מצות פרייה ורבייה, וכל אחד ואחד היה גודר את עצמו לפי מה שהיה מכיר את טבעו ורואה במה תקנתו.

וכן אמרו בהגדה על ענין היצר, אברהם השלים עמו ועליו נאמר ברצות ה' דרכי איש גם אויביו ישלים אתו, דוד עשה עמו מלחמה וראה שלא היה יכול לעמוד בו עמד עליו והרגו שנאמר וליבי חלל בקרבי. פי' אברהם השלים עמו היה יצרו רך וטבעו נח וערב שלא היה צריך לעשות עמו מלחמה כמו שאמרו בנדרים בתחלה אברם שלא היה מולך אלא על רמ"ג איברים ולבסוף אברהם שהמליכו על

saw he was unable to stand it, and it[24] killed him, as he said, "My heart is *chalal* [a corpse, an empty space] within me" [*Tehilim* 109:22].[25]

Avraham, who perfected his people, had a soft inclination and a calm, sweet nature – there was no need to contend with him, as the rabbis said [*Nedarim* 32b] that originally Avram ruled over 243 organs and later when he circumcised himself, *Hashem* gave him rulership of five more – two eyes, two ears, and his male organ.

David had a tough, strong *yetzer* that he had to conduct war with every day. Since the *yetzer* saw he couldn't win, he stood over David and killed him.[26] Some interpret "killing" as fasting and sackcloth, and others say it means he separated from women completely, for he saw that permissible sex [in excess] could subvert him to forbidden sex. We said before that a man has an organ that when satisfied gets hungry[27] [*Sanhedrin* 107a]. Whichever interpretation, when he saw his *yetzer* overcome him, he set his face to defeat it and to wage war against it, till he subdued it and cut it out.

The same applies to all of us as we recognize our evil inclination. I see the good path to subdue the *yetzer* – minimizing pleasure and benefit from food and drink. He may benefit from good aromas and warm water for washing. The small quantity of food can be sweet and spicy and well prepared, and his soul will accept it completely, but he will leave aside some, so as not to totally satisfy his desire. His wine should be well diluted so that he not become confused. The rabbis said to draw your hand away from a satisfying meal [*Gittin* 70a]. All these ways of moderation improve a person in two ways – preventing damage from excessive satisfaction of his desires and subduing the evil inclination and breaking the desire that generates it.

This discussion of eating and drinking may be applied to all the benefits and pleasures of the world – he should not completely fulfill his desires and, needless to say, those that may injure him. He might sin and pursue his desires and not

רמ"ח איברים שהוסיפו לו ממשלה על שתי אזנים ועל שתי עינים ועל הגויה. אבל דוד היה יצרו חזק וקשה והיה צריך לעשות עמו מלחמה בכל יום וכיון שראה שלא היה יכול לעמוד בו עמד עליו והרגו. יש מי שפירש הרגו בשקים ובתעניות. ויש מי שפירש שפירש מן האשה לגמרי כי ראה שמתוך ההיתר הסיתו על האסור. ובין כדברי זה ובין כדברי זה כיון שראה את יצרו מתגבר עליו שם את פניו להכניעו ונלחם עמו עד שהכניעו והכריתו.

וכן כל האדם צריך לעשות כן כל אחד ואחד לפי מה שהוא מכיר את טבעו. ואני רואה הגדר הגדול והשמור המעולה והדרך הטוב להכנעת היצר הוא רעבון הנפש ממעוט הנאותיה ותענוגיה במאכל ובמשתה, רק שיהנה מן הריח הטוב ורחיצת החמין לפי שהחמין ערבין עליו והמאכל המעט שיאכל יהא מתוקן ומתובל יפה בעבור אשר יערב עליו ותהיה נפשו מקבלתו ומפוייסות במועט ממנו, ולעולם יניח מעט מכדי צרכו ומהשלמת תאותו, ולא ישתה יין כי אם מזוג מזג יפה כדי שלא תטרף דעתו עליו, ועל זה אמרו רבותינו ז"ל סעודה שהנאתך משוך ידך ממנה ושתי תקנות גדולות יש בענין הזה, האחת שלא תזיקנו אכילתו, והשנית כי היא כניעת היצר ושברון התאוה.

כמו שאמרו בסעודה כן הדרך לכל הנאות העולם ותענוגיו שלא ימלא האדם מהם כל תאותו. ואין צ"ל שישמור האדם את עצמו מן המאכלים שהוא מכיר שהן מזיקין אותו, כי האוכל מאכלים המזיקים אותו ואפשר לו זולתן הרי זה פושע בגופו ופושע בנפשו מפני שהוא הולך אחר תאותו ואינו חושש על אבידת גופו והיא דרך היצה"ר ועצתו הסכלית להסיתו מדרך החיים אל דרך המות.

---

24. The evil inclination which is the same as the Angel of Death.

25. A completely different take on this in the midrash interprets *chalal*, as empty space, meaning that he conquered his *yetzer*. David asked why not say "the God of David along with God of Abraham Isaac and Jacob"? *Hashem* answered "They were tested, you weren't." David said, "Test me!" That night he sinned with Batsheva.

26. *Bava Basra* 16a: He descends, causes man to err, ascends, prosecutes, takes permission, then snatches the soul. "He" is at once the sin, the Satan, the snake, the evil inclination, the prosecutor, and the Angel of Death.

27. Think sex addiction.

be concerned with the destruction of his body – this is the way of the evil inclination and its foolish advice, to turn him aside from the path of life to the path of death.

All humanity knows that the evil inclination employs the permissible, and opens the door to sin in this manner, and if a person guards the door he does not need to worry. It is bad advice to fulfill his desire through permissible activity, for if he accustoms himself to completely satisfy himself with the permissible, his soul will be seeking this satisfaction all the time – to be prepared to turn to a mild transgression, and on from the mild to the severe. This is why he must be careful not to overdo the permissible, to limit himself somewhat not to allow his *yetzer* to turn him aside to the forbidden.

If one's heart desires a forbidden thing one should immediately think, is it not obvious if I would forbid myself a permissible desire, certainly I would forbid myself a forbidden desire. Then I would perish the thought and ever more so the deed. A person should not cause himself pain, lest it cause weakening of the heart, corrupt his deeds and his nature, and confuse his mind. His loss is greater than his reward, for he will lose his opportunity to study Torah and pray. If he studies, his Torah will be unsettled and he will not agree to the accepted *halacha* and interpretation, for Torah is only obtained through happiness. A person should not refrain from rejoicing in *mitzvah*, and from all pleasure of *mitzvah*, but keep his eyes trained against the *yetzer* and be careful not to completely fulfill all he desires. If he feels uneasy from a diminished diet, it is better that he eats small quantities more often than to fill his belly at once. If he senses in his nature a need to fast once or twice a week, he should fast. If he fasts out of need, he is called holy, as long as it does not interfere with his Torah study or observance of *mitzvot*.

The rabbis permitted him to take an oath to more stringently limit him from sin, as Boaz said in the matter of Rut, "I swear by my life; sleep till morning" [*Rut* 3:13]. The sages said that the *yetzer* taunted him the whole night, saying, "You are *panui*

וידע כל חי מדבר שאין דרך ליצה"ר עליו אלא מדרך ההיתר, ופתח דרכו מן המותר אצלו, ואם ישמור את הפתח אינו צריך שימור אחר. וכבר ערכתי הכל לפניך בתחלת השער הזה, כי דרך היועץ הבליעל ההוא יועצו למלאות תאותו מן המותר לו, ואחרי הרגילו אותו למלא תאותו בהיתר והשיא נפשו להיות שוקקה כל עת ולהיותה עורגת אל רעבונה אז יסיתנה אל האסור הקל ומן הקל אל החמור כאשר אמרתי לך. ועל זה הזהר בהיתר, ואם תגדור בו את עצמך ותמעט תאותך מן המותר לך מובטח אתה שלא יסיתך עוד יצרך אל האסור.

כי אם יעלה על לבך דבר אסור מיד אתה נושא קל וחומר לעצמך במותר לי נאסרתי באסור לי לא כ"ש, וכיון שאתה נושא ק"ו זה עליך מובטח לך שאתה פורש מן ההרהור וכ"ש מן המעשה. ואל יתענה אדם ענוי נפש פן יחלש לבו ויתקלקלו מעשיו וטבעיו ויתערבב מוחו ויהיה הפסדו מרובה משכרו כי יבטל מן התורה ומן התפלה, ואם ילמד לא תהיה תורתו מיושבת ולא יסכים להלכה ולפלפול השמועה, לפי שאין התורה נקנית אלא מתוך שמחה. ואל ימנע אדם עצמו מכל שמחת מצוה ומכל הנאת מצוה רק שיהיו עיניו פקוחות כנגד היצר ויהיה נזהר עליו פן ימלא כל תאותיו. ואם יחלש לבו על מיעוט אכילתו טוב לו שיאכל שני פעמים ביום מעט ואל ימלא כריסו בפעם אחת, ואם לא יזדמן לו לאכול שני פעמים ביום יהיה לו מן המרקחות המישבות את הלב, ויאכל מהן מעט ויתחזק לבו. גם אם יראה בעצמו ובטבעו שיהא צריך להתענות יום או יומים בשבוע יתענה לפי תקנתו, כי היושב בתענית והוא צריך לו נקרא קדוש, ובלבד שלא יבטל מן התורה ומן המצות בעבורו.

גם השבועה שהיא חמורה התירוה לגדור את עצמו בה מן העבירה כאשר אמר בועז בענין רות חי ה' שכבי עד הבוקר. אמרו חכמים שהיה יצרו מקטרג עליו כל הלילה ואומר לו אתה פנוי והיא פנויה והאשה נקנית לך בבעילה לך ובעלה ותהיה קנויה לך בבעילה, קפץ בועז ונשבע כנגד היצר חי ה' אם אעשה זאת ולאשה אמר שכבי עד הבקר.

כן כל האדם יוכל לדעת בעצמו הגדר שהוא טוב לו אם הכניעה או השבועה, ואני רואה שאין טוב מן הכניעה ורעבון הנפש כאשר אמרתי. ואם יצטרך עוד אל השבועה ישבע ויקיים בענין שאמר דוד נשבעתי ואקיימה לשמור משפטי צדקך.

[permissible, available] and so is she, and you can marry her by intercourse" [*Vayikra Rabba* 23:11]. Boaz jumped and swore to oppose the *yetzer*, "I swear by my life I will not do this," then told the woman, "Sleep till morning."

All people know on their own which *geder* [fence, limit] is good for them, submission [like fasting] or oath, and I sense the best is submission and the hunger of the soul, as I said. If he needs more [to keep him from sin], he should swear an oath, as David said, "I swore and I establish to guard the judgments of your righteousness" [*Tehilim* 119:101].

The main fence is to guard his eyes not to look at that which is not his, and to just limit this makes him modest and abashed [in the favorable sense], like the man with a lame wife who died without him ever noticing. How modest was he! [*Shabbat* 53b]. If he guards his eyes, his heart will be guarded, thus all of him will be guarded. Three senses complete the sin – vision, thought, and touch. A fourth sense, hearing, is not nearly as close as vision to reaching the heart and sense of thought and subsequently the sense of touch. This is why the verse teaches us not to turn aside to the heart and eyes and the rabbis said that the eye and the heart are vehicles of sin [*Yerushalmi Bereishit* 1:5]. Shlomo said, "My son, give me your heart, and let your eyes observe my ways" [Prov. 23:26]. Also, in midrash, "Give me your heart and your eyes, and I will know you are mine" [*Yerushalmi Bereishit* 1:5]. The first of all the firsts, He knew man and his *yetzer*, and that he should recognize his potential and give his heart to the One he serves and fears, and whose commandment he should do, as David said to Shlomo, "Know the God of your father, and serve Him with a full heart" [*Divrei Hayamim I* 28:9].

And though He is hidden from the eyes of the living, He is found in the hearts of all life and revealed in their thoughts. Every creature knows there is no separating from the One who forms us,[28] yet there is no connection to Him.[29] For all connections are limiting, and the Creator, may He be exalted, has none of these features, and He is the origin of everything,

והראש לכל הגדרים שישמור האדם את עיניו מכל מה שאינו שלו, ואף אם ימעט ראייתו ממה שהוא שלו אז יקרא צנוע ובייש, כענין שאמרו על אותו האיש שהיתה אשתו חגרת ולא הכיר בה כל ימיו ואמרו עליו כמה צנוע אדם זה שלא הכיר באשתו. ואם ישמור את עיניו נמצא ליבו שמור, ומתוך שיהיו עיניו ולבו שמורים נמצא כולו שמור, כי על ידי שלשה חושים שבאדם העון נגמר, והם הראות, והמחשבה, והמשוש. ואם יש בו החוש הרביעי גם הוא משמש את המשוש והוא חוש השמע אינו קרוב לחוש המחשבה בכמו חוש הראות כי הוא מביא מיד אל חוש הלב וחוש הלב מביא אל המשוש. וע"ז הזהיר הכתוב ולא תתורו אחרי לבבכם ואחרי עיניכם ואמרו בהגדה עינא וליבא תרי סרסורי דחטאה אינון, וכן אמר החכם תנה בני לבך לי ועיניך דרכי תצורנה. ואמר הב לי לבך ועינך ואנא ידע דאת דילי. וראשון לכל הראשים כלם שידע האדם את יוצרו ויכיר את ברואו ויתן אל לבו למי יעבוד וממי יירא ומצות מי יעשה ומי הזהירו, כמו שאמר דוד לשלמה דע את אלהי אביך ועבדהו בלבב שלם.

ואם הוא נעלם מעיני כל חי אך הוא נמצא בלבבות ונגלה במחשבות, וידע כל נוצר שאינו נפרד מן היוצר ואינו מחובר לו, כי כל מחובר מוגבל, וכל מוגבל מחודש, והבורא יתעלה אין בו אחת מן מדות האלה, כי הוא קדמון לכל, לא מוגבל ולא מחודש, אף כי הבורא ברא את הנברא יש מאין, ואם יש מחפצו ומרצונו לעשות מצותו ולקבל שכרו אם טוב ואם רע אין ישותו חוצצת ולא מפרדת ולא מגבלת ולא ממעטת, כי הוא כאין נגדו בראשיתו ובקדמותו, והבורא יתעלה הוא מקום עולמו ואין עולמו מקומו, ותבנית הדבר כאשר העולם מלא מן האויר והכל נכנסין בתוך האויר נרגשין ממנו ואינו נראה להם, ואם דמה הכתוב האדם ביד הבורא כחומר ביד היוצר להשמיע את האוזן מה שהיא יכולה לשמוע, אך רחוק המשל מן המליצה כרחוק מזרח ממערב.

כי היוצר העושה מלאכת החומר אעפ"י שעושה את הכלי קדם למלאכת הכלי זה החומר שממנו נעשה הכלי קודם לאומן, ועל כן מעשה ידי האומן חוצצין לפניו ומפרידין בינותיו וממעטין ראות עיניו ודוחקין עליו, אך הבורא יתברך ויתעלה לא קדמו דבר, ויש מאין ברא הכל, ועל כן אין לפניו חוצץ ולא מפריד, ועל כן החי יתן אל לבו כי הוא רואה את בוראו מה שאין עיניו רואות, ואם יחטאו הידים והרגלים ושאר

without limitation,[30] creating His world, existence out of non-existence, something from nothing.

If a person has the will and desire to do His *mitzvot* and receive recompense, his existence is not divided or separated or limited or minimized. For he is insignificant compared to Him at his beginning[31] and his origin, and the Creator, may He be exalted, is the Place of His world,[32] and not the world His place [BR 68:10]. In the descriptive analogy, people enter the air of the world and feel it but do not see it. Consider the notion that man is in the hand of the Creator like clay in the hand of the potter, to make him aware of his circumstance. The allegory is far from the subject as east is from west. If man in the Creator's hand is like clay in the potter's hand, it is merely a way to make it understood [*l'hashmia*] by the ear.

Before the potter who formed and worked the clay, was the clay itself, created out of nothing by the Creator, may He be blessed. Before Him there is no division or separation. Therefore, the living creature inserts in his heart that he is seeing the Creator in a way the eye cannot sense. If he errs and lets his hands and legs and the other parts of the body sin without the heart's intent, and eats whatever comes into his hand, assuming it is permissible, he is like the blind. Similarly, if one spits at another not knowing the other is there across from him, he does not deserve to be punished. But if he sees that what is in his hand is forbidden and he eats it or sees the man in front of him and spits at him, will he not be severely punished? Thus, one who sins in heart and thought while perceiving his Creator with the power of reason and intention, yet still sins against Him shamelessly and brazenly and without embarrassment before His honor, how great is his punishment! A man who transgresses the command of a human king to his face will have his punishment doubled and redoubled as compared to one who transgresses secretly.

And now, son of man, pay attention to all these things, observe their details, and hear them with your ears. Observe and you will see He who formed you standing before you and see

איברי הגוף בלא כוונת הלב הנה הם שוגגים בעבור כי הם כסומא שאינו רואה ואוכל מה שבא לידו בחזקת היתר, או כי ירוק כנגד האדם מבלי ידיעה כי לא היה יודע שהיה אדם עומד כנגדו, ואינו ראוי להענישו, אך מי שהוא רואה מה שהוא תופס בידו ואם הוא דבר האסור ואוכל אותו ואם יעמוד אדם נגדו וירק בפניו הלא נענש על אלה עונש גדול, כן חטאת הלב והמחשבה כי הם רואים את בוראם בכח כוונתם ושכלם, ואם יחטאו כנגדו ולא יבושו ממנו ולא יכלמו מפני כבוד בוראם העומד לנגדם ויעיזו פניהם לפני יוצרם כמה גדול עונשם, כאדם שעובר על מצות המלך בפניו שהעונש שלו מרובה ונכפל ממי שהוא נסתר ממנו ועובר על מצותו.

ואתה בן אדם שים לבך לכל הדברים האלה וראה תכונתם, ובאזניך שמע ואת עיניך תפקח ותראה תמונת יוצרך העומדת לפניך נגדך, וראה כי הוא בשמים ואתה על הארץ ונשמרת מכל דבר רע. תניא ונשמרת מכל דבר רע שלא יהרהר אדם ביום ויבא לידי טומאה בלילה, מכאן א"ר פנחס בן יאיר חסידות מביאה לידי זריזות, זריזות מביאה לידי נקיות, נקיות מביאה לידי טהרה, טהרה מביאה לידי רוח הקדש, רוח הקדש מביאה לידי תחיית המתים, תחיית המתים באה על ידי אליהו

28. Perhaps in the sense of "There is nothing but Him" [Deut. 4:35]. Man is in and part of His Universe.

29. Perhaps in the sense of man's independence via free choice. To achieve connection with Him man must first manifest His Will through his free choice and rise to *devekut*, sublime connection.

30. Creation is perpetual renewal, and man is constantly recreated, but not the Creator Himself. In the *shema* blessing we say, "He renews creation with His goodness perpetually."

31. Tanya: All before Him is of no significance.

32. *Devarim* 4:39: *Hashem* is God in the heavens above and on the earth below, nothing else exists but Him. *Bereishit Rabba* 68:10: And he [Yaakov] encountered the Place [*Bereishit* 28:10] means that he wanted to pass, but the whole world became a wall in front of him.

that He is in the heavens and you are on earth, and you will be guarded from any evil thing [*Devarim* 23:10]. A person should not contemplate an evil thing by day and come to impurity by night. From here, Rabbi Pinchas ben Yair learned that *chasidut* [saintliness] brings about *zerizut* [zeal], which brings about cleanliness, which brings about purity, which brings about the Holy Spirit, which brings about the resurrection of the dead, which comes through Eliyahu, may he be remembered for good [*Yerushalmi Shekalim* 3:3].[33] *Zehirut* [watchfulness] is what one should take care to keep before he comes to do a deed. *Zerizut* [zeal] at the time of the deed is the way to perform a commandment enthusiastically and not with laziness. If he has an opportunity to sin, he should flee and separate himself from it zealously. *Nekiut* is cleanliness of body and clothing, as the rabbis said that any Torah scholar who has a stain on himself must die [*Shabbat* 114a]. Purity is understood to be the absence of *tuma*, such that one should take care not to become *tamei.* If a Kohen should touch an impure object, he must purify himself to eat in a state of purity. *Kedusha* is the sanctity of the heart and thought. Saintliness is to act beyond the letter of the law in every matter. The reason for all these things is found in the scriptures. Rabbi Yoshaya said in the name of Rabbi Meir that anyone established in the Land of Israel who speaks the holy tongue and eats his *chulin* [non-sanctified ordinary meat] in a state of purity, and reads the *shema* prayer morning and evening, is certain to be a son of the World-to-Come.

We have completed the Book of Holiness. Praise and thanks to He who created His world in six days.

זכור לטוב. הזהירות הוא שאדם נזהר ונשמר קודם שיבא מעשה לידו. והזריזות היא בשעת מעשה שיעשה מצותו בזריזות ולא על ידי דרך עצלות, ואם יבא חטא לידו יברח ויפרד ממנו בזריזות. הנקיות היא נקיות גופו ובגדיו מן הלכלוך כענין שאמרו כל תלמיד חכם שנמצא רבב על בשרו חייב מיתה. הטהרה היא באה מכלל הטומאות שישמור עצמו מן הטומאות ואם יגע בהן יטהר עצמו ויאכל חוליו בטהרה. קדושה היא קדושת הלב והמחשבה כאשר אמרנו. חסידות הוא עושה לפנים משורת הדין בכל דבר נקרא חסיד. וכל אלה מפורש טעמם מן המקראות. בשקלים ירושלמי תני בשם ר׳ מאיר כל הקבוע בארץ ישראל ומדבר בלשון הקודש ואוכל את חוליו בטהרה וקורא את שמע בבקר ובערב יהא מבושר שהוא בן עולם הבא.

השלמנו ספר הקדושה. שבח והודאה לבורא עולמו בששה.

---

33. *Avodah Zarah* 20b: Pinchas ben Yair learned that Torah leads to watchfulness, leading to zeal, leading to cleanliness, leading to separation, leading to purity, leading to saintliness, leading to humility, leading to fear of sin, leading to holiness, leading to revival of the dead. On this, Rabbi Moshe Chaim Luzzato wrote *Mesilat Yesharim*, *The Path of the Just*, the major work of the ethical movement 1500 years after Rabbi Pinchas and 700 years after Raavad.

A Response to *The Holy Gate*

Excerpts (in English) from
Sela HaMachloket (Stone of Dispute)
by Baal HaMor, Rabbi Zerachia HaLevi

שער הקדושה.
כולו יפה ונעים.
תמים דעים בדעת שעשועים.
להסיר מעשה תעתועים.
ולהיישר מעשה צעצועים.
אבל אין מוסרין דברי צניעות כי אם לצנועים.
ועל זה נאמר [משלי יא:ב] ואת צנועים חכמה.

The Holy Gate, is beautiful and pleasant in its entirety,
Pure of knowledge in its amusements
Removing deceitful deeds
Rectifying playful acts
But modest words are to be given over
Only to the modest, on which it said:
"When pride comes, disgrace follows,
But with modesty comes wisdom."

[From the new notes of the Baal HaMor]:

In *The Holy Gate* of Rabbi Avraham, we see something unfit for his holy tongue to utter, and not for the pure of eyes to see. "Who knows the spirit of the sons of man? Does it ascend upward? And the spirit of the animal, does it descend downward to the earth" [*Kohelet* 3:21]? Only the Creator realizes the level of virtue of souls. Rabbi Avraham interprets that even if that level of holiness were amazingly high, different souls would still comprehend on a different level, for the wise and the fools are not equal in consciousness. Therefore, it is not for us to decide who is worthy to read these words.

It seems from this that Rabbi Avraham did not see the words of the great philosopher [Rambam], who said that a great person can discern any depth of meaning and reveal any unknown. This level of virtue has great and strong signs and wonders. Therefore, God forbid such an interpretation of this verse.

When the verse of *Kohelet* says, "Who knows," it is to magnify our view of the sages who know this level of virtue. *Kohelet* says, "Who is like the wise and who knows the interpretation of a word?" [*Kohelet* 8:1]. Only the wisest and most virtuous are fit to see this holy work.

Thanks and praises to the One who has greatness,
The reason of all reasons and the cause of all causes,
Who has no beginning and no end,
He hears prayer, to prepare action, and improve a word.
Jewish character is enormous, I raise a gift to Him,
Among the stones of dispute, we will be
To Avraham and to Zerachia,
Like a doe and like a gazelle in doubled redemption,
My brother with me will bless *Hashem*,
Because I contested with him, he will bless *Hashem*.

The Prayer on the Night of Intimacy (in English)

by the Kabbalah Master Ramban
(Rabbenu Moshe ben Nachman)

May it be Your will, Creator of all the worlds, Righteous in all the generations, for the sake of Your Great Name, which arises from the verse, "*Hashem*, bless our remembrance," a new seed, a holy seed, acceptable and proper, good and beautiful, corrected and received. And fitting to live and endure without sin and shame. And bless me in Your Name, and bless my home with Your Remembrance, and may I know that my tent is at peace and may You draw out the continuance of my seed and the wellsprings of the source of Israel. Purify my body and sanctify my soul and my thoughts and my spirit and my awareness and my feelings that I be strengthened and enclothed in Your good, pure, giving Spirit in order to perfect my accomplishment of Your Will. And perfect my seed, that it be built and live, and act in truth and honesty to complete and establish Your Will with tastefulness and grace and kindness, in health and strength and power. And there should not be defect or damage or illness or pain or weakness. And they shall not lack of goodness all the days of their life. And bless me and my home [wife] and my offspring with all that perfects our knowledge, our spirituality, and our feelings to do all our deeds according to Your Will. And bless me with the blessings of heaven above, blessings of the deep that crouches below, and the house of Your servant will be blessed from Your blessings forever. Amen forever, Selah.

Kegavna Prayer

(*Zohar Trumah* 134:1)

JUST AS THEY (all six *sefiros*) unite above in Oneness, she (the *sefira* of Kingship) unites below in the secret of Oneness so that it may join those above, the Oneness below paralleling the Oneness above. The Holy One, Blessed be He, Who is One above, does not sit on His royal Throne of Glory until it (Kingship below) is made over in the secret of Oneness like His, that there may be a Oneness parallel to a Oneness. Thus, we have set forth the secret of *Hashem* (Who is above) is One and His name (i.e., His Kingship below) is One.

This is the secret of the Sabbath: She (Kingship) is called "Sabbath" when she becomes united in the secret of Oneness so that *Hashem*'s Oneness may rest upon her, [i.e., during] the evening prayer of the Sabbath, for then the holy Throne of Glory becomes unified through the secret of Oneness, and becomes ready for the Supreme Holy King to rest upon it. When the Sabbath arrives, she unified herself in Oneness and divests herself of the Other Side (evil), all harsh judgments are removed from her, and she remains alone with the Oneness of the holy light. She crowns herself with many crowns for the Holy King. All wrathful dominions and bearers of grievance flee together, and there is no power but her in all the worlds. Her face glows with a heavenly light and she takes the holy people below as her crown, for they crown themselves with new souls (that arrive with the Sabbath). Then their prayers begin by blessing her with joy and with radiant faces.

Bless Hashem the Blessed One....

תפילת כגוונא

(זוהר תרומה קל"ד:א)

כְּגַוְנָא דְאִנּוּן מִתְיַחֲדִין לְעֵלָּא בְּאֶחָד. אוּף הָכִי אִיהִי אִתְיַחֲדַת לְתַתָּא בְּרָזָא דְאֶחָד לְמֶהֱוֵי עִמְּהוֹן לְעֵלָּא חָד לָקֳבֵל חָד. קוּדְשָׁא בְּרִיךְ הוּא אֶחָד. לְעֵלָּא לָא יָתִיב עַל כּוּרְסַיָּא דִיקָרֵיהּ עַד דְאִתְעֲבִידַת אִיהִי בְּרָזָא דְאֶחָד. כְּגַוְנָא דִילֵיהּ לְמֶהֱוֵי אֶחָד בְּאֶחָד. וְהָא אוּקִימְנָא רָזָא דַיְ-הוָה אֶחָד וּשְׁמוֹ אֶחָד:

רָזָא דְשַׁבָּת אִיהִי שַׁבָּת דְאִתְאַחֲדַת בְּרָזָא דְאֶחָד. לְמִשְׁרֵי עֲלָהּ רָזָא דְאֶחָד. צְלוֹתָא דְמַעֲלֵי שַׁבְּתָא דְהָא אִתְאַחֲדַת כּוּרְסַיָּא יַקִּירָא קַדִּישָׁא בְּרָזָא דְאֶחָד. וְאִתְתַּקָּנַת לְמִשְׁרֵי עֲלָהּ מַלְכָּא קַדִּישָׁא עִלָּאָה. כַּד עַיִּל שַׁבְּתָא אִיהִי אִתְיַחֲדַת וְאִתְפַּרְשַׁת מִסִּטְרָא אַחֲרָא. וְכָל דִּינִין מִתְעַבְּרִין מִנָּהּ וְאִיהִי אִשְׁתְּאָרַת בְּיִחוּדָא דִנְהִירוּ קַדִּישָׁא. וְאִתְעַטְּרַת בְּכַמָּה עִטְרִין לְגַבֵּי מַלְכָּא קַדִּישָׁא. וְכָל שׁוּלְטָנֵי רוּגְזִין וּמָארֵי דְדִינָא כֻּלְּהוּ עַרְקִין וְאִתְעַבְרוּ מִנָּהּ. וְלֵית שׁוּלְטָנָא אַחֲרָא בְּכֻלְּהוּ עָלְמִין (בַּר מִנָּהּ). וְאַנְפָּהָא נְהִירִין בִּנְהִירוּ עִלָּאָה וְאִתְעַטְּרַת לְתַתָּא בְּעַמָּא קַדִּישָׁא. וְכֻלְּהוֹן מִתְעַטְּרִין בְּנִשְׁמָתִין חַדְתִּין כְּדֵין שֵׁירוּתָא דִצְלוֹתָא. לְבָרְכָא לָהּ בְּחֶדְוָה בִּנְהִירוּ דְאַנְפִּין.

ברכו את ה' המבורך....

The Blessing of Intimate Relations (in English)

from the Siddur of Rabbi Yaakov Emden

WHY DID OUR RABBIS not establish a blessing for conjugal relations, neither a blessing acknowledging benefit or pleasure, like for food, nor a blessing on fulfillment of a commandment, like circumcision? The answer is they intended the words of the blessing on going to sleep [*hamapil*] to suffice for the pleasure of intimate relations with the inclusion of "Let my bed be *shlema* [complete, perfect] before You." This includes an intention to pray to *Hashem* for the perfection of the seed as well as a prayer that he not waste seed during sleep. If he blesses the sleep blessing [*hamapil*], then sleeps, then wakes and has relations with his wife, he need not repeat the blessing.

The great Kabbala master the Arizal [Rabi Yitzchak Luria, 16th Century Safed] said it is good to recite *Tehilim* 23, "*Hashem* is my shepherd, I shall not want" before marital relations, just as one says it before the third Shabbat meal, which represents the conjugal union of *Bina* and *Tiferet*, for both have the same aspect.

אגרת הקודש לרמב"ן
THE HOLY LETTER

אגרת הקודש [ששלח הרמב"ן ז"ל לאחד החברים בענין חבור האדם אל אשתו]

attributed to Ramban
(Rabbenu Moshe ben Nachman)

Introduction to *The Holy Letter*

BY MOSHE KUHR

IGERET HAKODESH – *The Holy Letter*, is a pure and holy treatment of the matter of intimacy and sexuality. Since modesty and privacy are paramount Torah values, matters between husband and wife have been historically relegated to esoteric texts not accessible to the general population, or even Torah scholars who do not take the initiative to pursue their study. As a result, most learn about intimacy and sexuality from the profane secular world. The holiness that permeates the Torah view of the precious relationship of man and wife remains under wraps. The same could be said for our precious Kabbala lore for some of the same reasons. It is true that the subject matter is inappropriate for children and that it may fall into the hands of those who might misuse it, but the views of our sages, of blessed memory, need to see the light of day. The void created by hiding the Torah view of sexuality in our time is quickly filled by the pervasive licentious media and social culture that presents all the wrong imagery and messages.

Consider a Jewish person growing up in a non-Torah environment. He is titillated by seductive imagery from the time he is aware of it, and the message is that pleasure is to be pursued. The pursuit of "happiness" is up there on the scale of values with liberty and life itself. At the same time, he, like Adam and Eve, is aware of the shameful, sinful aspect of intimacy. Christianity's view is that the Original Sin is sex. A superficial perusal of the

Bible could lead one to believe *Hashem* may disapprove, given the prominence of restrictions of incest, harlotry, *nidah*, adultery, etc. Marriage law appears in the context of divorce. The positive commandment of pleasuring one's wife is hidden in the laws of the female Israelite bondservant. So the person assumes that sexuality is outside the bounds of our faith.

Now consider a young person growing up in a Torah environment. He is instructed to avoid contamination by the sexuality that permeates the general culture but we know it happens anyway. He is guided away from Torah texts deemed inappropriate. Not only is the Rashi on Adam's naming the animals expunged, but even high school graduates tell me they skipped the Yehuda and Tamar chapter. He learns the "thou shalt nots" but fails to be properly prepared for courtship and marriage.

This text, *The Holy Letter*, should be required learning of every maturing Jew and should be a leading feature of any effort to present Torah to the uninitiated.

Authorship

Extant manuscripts that form the basis of our versions of *The Holy Letter* contain no reference to the author, but tradition attributes it to Rabbenu Moshe ben Nachman, the Ramban (1194–1272), of Gerona, Aragon, Spain. Seventy years after his death, the work was included in Yisrael Alnakava's *Menorat Hamaor,* this time attributed to the Ramban.

The problem with this attribution is that *Igeret Hakodesh* is discordant with Ramban's other writings in both style and content. Ramban was the Torah leader of his time, a time of the emergence of Kabbala. He gathered the greatest scholars of Spain and Provence, like Rabbenu Bachya, Rabbenu Yona, Rashba, and Recanati to his *kollel* in Gerona, but his writings are not openly Kabbalistic as is *The Holy Letter*. In his commentary on the Torah, he occasionally quotes a difficult Zohar without explanation and cryptically notes, "he who understands will understand." This sharply contrasts with the Kabbalistic style of *The Holy Letter*.

Rabbi Dr. Charles Chavel, of blessed memory, the preeminent scholar of the works of the Ramban, collected, translated, annotated, and published many of the Ramban's works in Hebrew and English. In the second volume of the Hebrew edition of *Kitvei HaRamban* [Mossad Harav Kook, Jerusalem, 1964], the *Igeret Hakodesh* appears, meticulously edited and sourced from several manuscripts. The introduction discusses the authorship at length and concludes it is unlikely Ramban wrote it. For example, the main thesis of the text, that sexual intimacy is noble and holy, is contradicted explicitly in Ramban's commentary on *Vayikra* 18:10.

Another line of evidence suggests who the true author might be. Rabbenu Menachem Recanati, Kabbalist and student of Ramban, brings word for word a large segment of *The Holy Letter* in his commentary on *Devarim* 24:5 without attribution. Elsewhere he is careful to credit his teacher when the latter's work is cited, and Chavel shows that Recanati's unattributed comments are always his own.

Note: Following each chapter, I have added a comment, introduced with my initials "MDK."

My dear student:
May *Hashem* bless you and keep you
My brother who is like my soul
That you care to investigate the ways
Whence to know the fear of *Hashem*
And to go in the way of the illuminating light
Across from the pure *Menorah*
To be saved from the dark path
That causes the blind to stumble
Those who never saw
The lights of warning.
Now you ask me to teach you the way
By which a person could fulfill his needs
That all would be for the sake of heaven
In the matter of intimacy between man and his wife
In order to merit sons worthy of teaching Torah
Fit to receive the yoke of the Kingdom of Heaven
And as I see your thoughts proceeding
To the true path
I will want to open for you
The gates of righteousness in the matter
In order that you reach your proper intent
In the faithful Torah of *Hashem*.
To quickly fulfill your request
That a table be set before you.
I will arrange the matter in six chapters
Corresponding to the six branches of the *Menorah*.

יברכך ה' וישמרך.
אחי בהיותך זריז ומהיר לחקור על הדרכים אשר מהם תדע ידיעת יראת ה' יתברך,
ותוכל ללכת בדרכי האמת ובדרך האורה המאירה,
אל מול פני המנורה יאירו,
כדי שתנצל מדרך האפלה
המכשלת את העורים אשר לא ראו פני המאורות המזהירות,
הנה בקשת ממני אחי להורות לך הדרך שבה יוכל האדם לעשות צרכיו ויהיו כולם לשם שמים בענין חבור האדם אל אשתו, כדי לזכות לבנים בעלי הוראה
ראויים לקבל את עול מלכות שמים. ובראותי מחשבותיך שהלכת על דרך האמת,
אני אראה לך שערי צדק
בענין שתשיג הכוונה בתורת השם יתעלה הנאמנה.
וכדי שתשיג בקשתך מהם,
אסדר לך דברים פרקים מסודרים.
ואקדים לך הקדמות בזה הפרק.

Chapter One

A Letter to My Dear Student

KNOW AND UNDERSTAND, that the Nation of Israel is separate, lofty, and unique for *Hashem*, may He be blessed, as the prophet said [*Yeshayahu* 43:21], "I created this nation for Myself, that they should tell My praise." When we say [*Shmuel* II, 7:23, Shabbat *Mincha Amida*], "You are One and Your Name is One, and who is like Your nation, Israel, a singular people on earth," we are saying He has separated us to be uniquely His for His *kavod* [goodness, glory], as He said [*Vayikra* 20:26], "And I will separate you from the nations to be Mine." Servants conduct themselves according to the conduct they see in their masters. *Hashem* is our Master and we are His servants, and He who is the ultimate in holiness has commanded us to be holy as He is holy [*Vayikra* 19:2]. Furthermore, when we are told [*Devarim* 28:9] "And you should walk in His ways," the rabbis have explained [*Shabbos* 133b], "Be holy in the way He is holy, be freely giving in the way He is freely giving, etc." If so, Israel needs to be firmly grounded in His fundamental principles in order that they resemble Him in all their deeds, as *Hashem* said [*Vayikra11*:48], "And you should make yourselves holy and be holy for I am holy."

If this is done, it will be found that whenever we do the good and the honest thing, we will sanctify His great Name, as it is said [*Devarim* 4:7], "For which is a great nation that has a God Who is close to it...and which great nation has righteous decrees

דע כי בהיות אומת ישראל מיוחדת להקב"ה והבדילה בתורתו הקדושה מכל האומות כאשר הוא יתברך נבדל מכל מה שזולתו, כאומרו יתברך (ישעיה מג כא) עם זו יצרתי לי ואמר במקום אחר (ישעיהו מב כד) ה' (אחד) [זו חטאנו לו] לגזרה שוה. וזה שאנו אומרים אתה אחד ושמך אחד ומי כעמך ישראל גוי אחד. ואחר כך אמר יצרתי לי כלומר הבדלתי לי להיות מיוחד לכבודי כאמרו (ויקרא כ כו) ואבדיל אתכם מן העמים להיות לי. וכבר ידעת כי העבדים הנהגתם כפי מה שהם רואים בהנהגת אדוניהם, והוא יתברך שהוא אדוננו ואנחנו עבדיו הנה הוא קדוש שאין קדוש כמותו, וצוה לנו להיותנו קדושים כאשר הוא קדוש. ופי' רבותינו ז"ל (ספרי שם, סוטה יד א) בפסוק (דברים כח) והלכת בדרכיו מה הוא קדוש אף אתה היה קדוש מה הוא חנון אף אתה היה חנון. וא"כ נמצאו כל ישראל הנהגותיהם מיוחסת על יחוד השם הגדול יתברך, לפיכך מתדמין אליו בכל מעשיהן והוא יתברך אמר (ויקרא יא, מד) והתקדשתם והייתם קדושים כי קדוש אני ה'.

ומאחר שכל מעשינו כדמיון מעשה השם יתברך, נמצא שכל זמן שאנו עושין הטוב והישר, שאנו מקדשין שמו הגדול כאמרו (דברים ד) ומי גוי גדול אשר לו חקים ומשפטים צדיקים, לפי שאנו מתדמים לבוראנו יתברך. וכל זמן שלא נתנהג כשורה (וכל מעשינו) [ונעשה מעשים] מקולקלים, אנו מחללין בהם שם שמים, אחר שאנו מתדמים לו והנה מעשינו מכוערים. ועל זה אמרו במסכת יומא (פו א) בזמן

and ordinances such as this entire Torah?" We are constantly being compared to our Creator. Likewise, whenever we conduct ourselves improperly and our deeds are corrupted, we profane the Name of Heaven. On this the rabbis said [*Yoma* 86a], "If a person reads and learns Torah and conducts his business matters pleasantly in the marketplace, about him it is said [*Yeshayahu* 49:3], "You are Israel in whom I will be glorified." But whenever a person reads and learns Torah and his business affairs are improper, what do people say about him? "Did you see so and so the Torah scholar; how corrupt are his ways?" About him, the prophet says [*Yechezkel* 36:20], "This is the nation of God, and from their Land they departed," and the Name of Heaven is profaned. The sanctification of His exalted name or its profanation depends on our deeds.

The physical makeup of man and his nature are reasons for his being good or bad. The formation of his disposition follows his genetic makeup, a consequence of the drop of semen from which he came into being. The intimate act of a man and his wife is the reason for sanctifying or profaning *Hashem* through the children that will be born. He commanded us and warned us, and said we must make ourselves holy at the time of intimacy, as it is written [*Vayikra* 15:31], "And you shall warn the children of Israel against their impurity." This is the reason for the birth of righteous children who sanctify the Name of Heaven or evildoers who profane the Name of Heaven.

Therefore, you will need to know what the rabbis said a person must do, to make himself holy during the intimate act, and what is the nature of this holiness. I have divided it into five parts:

- The Nature of the Intimate Act
- The Timing of the Intimate Act
- Food and the Intimate Act
- Intent and the Intimate Act
- The Quality of the Intimate Act

שאדם קורא ושונה ומשאו ומתנו באמונה עליו הכתוב אומר (ישעיה מט) ויאמר לי עבדי אתה ישראל אשר בך אתפאר, אבל בזמן שאדם קורא ושונה ואין משאו ומתנו באמונה מה בני אדם אומרים עליו ראיתם פלוני כמה מקולקלין דרכיו ומעשיו ועליו הכתוב אומר (יחזקאל לו) עם ה' אלה ומארצו יצאו ונמצא שם שמים מתחלל. והטעם על כל זה שאמרנו כי מאחר שאנו מתדמין לו במעשינו הנה קדושת השם וחלולו תלוי במעשינו.

ואחר שהודענוך כל זה, דע כי בהיות החומר של אדם וטבעו סבת היותו רע או טוב מצד תכונת המזג כפי הטפה שנתהווה ממנה, ונמצא חיבורו סבת קדושת השם או חלולו כפי הבנים שיוליד, צוה אותנו על זה והזהירנו ואמר כי נצטרך לקדש עצמנו בשעת תשמיש כאשר באה הקבלה בפסוק (ויקרא טו) והזרתם את בני ישראל מטומאתם, ומפני שזו היא סבה להוליד אדם בנים צדיקים מקדשים שם שמים [או רשעים מחללים שם שמים.]

ואחר שהדבר כן, תצטרך לדעת מה שאמרנו כי צריך האדם לקדש עצמו בשעת תשמיש. וקדושה זו נחלקת לחמשה חלקים. הדרך הראשון, במהות החבור. הדרך השני, בזמן החבור. הדרך השלישי, במזון הראוי לחבור. הדרך הרביעי, בכונת החבור. הדרך החמישי, באיכות החיבור.

והנני נכנס לבאר הדברים בענין שיספיק לפי (הכוונה) [כונתך]. [ואביא] כל אחד [בפרק] המיוחד לו.

MDK: The author sets the stage in the first paragraph, relating in Hashem's words to Isaiah the purpose for which the world was and is being created.[1] The 611th commandment, to emulate Hashem, is the watchword for all human activity. All human activity has the potential to sanctify or profane Hashem's name. Certainly, this principle applies to sexual matters. The act of intimacy is a particularly sensitive moment, affecting the next and future generations, for it must be performed with holiness. How to achieve this holiness must be learned, the way all Torah matters are learned – through the words of the sages.

---

1. In the *Siddur*: "Who creates anew each day the act of creation."

Chapter Two

The Nature of the Intimate Act

Sexual intimacy can be carried out in one of two ways. One is a matter of holiness and dignity, done in an appropriate way, at a proper time, with proper intent. Do not think there is disgrace or ugliness, in proper intimacy, God forbid. Sexual intimacy is called, for good reason, *yedia*, knowledge, as in [*Shmuel I*, 1:19], "And Elkana knew his wife Chana."[2] The secret is the drop of seed drawn in holiness and purity from the place of knowledge and understanding which is the brain. If intimacy were not such a great and holy matter it would not be called *yedia*.

It is not like Rabbi Moshe ben Maimon, of blessed memory, held in the *Guide to the Perplexed* when he praised Aristotle for saying that the sense of touch and associated urges like eating, drinking, and intimacy are shameful to us. It cannot be as the Greek said, a saying that smacks of apostasy for someone who believes that the world is continually renewed with *Hashem*'s intent.

We children of the possessors of the holy Torah believe that *Hashem*, may He be blessed, created everything according to the decree of His wisdom, and He did not create anything ugly or disgraceful. If intimacy is disgraceful, then the sexual organs are also. He created them, as the Torah says [*Devarim* 32:6], "He made you and fashioned you" in form as well as function. When King Shlomo said [*Kohelet* 2:12], "What can a man do

הדרך הראשון - במהות החבור

דע כי חבור זה הוא ענין קדוש ונקי כשיהיה הדבר כפי מה שראוי ובזמן הראוי ובכוונה הנכונה. ואל יחשוב אדם כי בחבור הראוי יש גנאי וכיעור ח"ו. שהחבור הראוי נקרא ידיעה, ולא לחנם נקרא כך כאמור (ש"א א) וידע אלקנה את חנה אשתו. וזהו סוד טפת הזרע כשהיא נמשכת ממקום הקדושה ובטהרה נמשכת הדעה [והחכמה] והבינה והוא המוח. ודע שאלו לא היה בדבר קדושה גדולה לא היו קוראין אל החבור ידיעה.

[ואין הדבר כאשר חשב הרב המורה ז"ל במורה הנבוכים בהיותו משבח לארסט"ו על מה שאמר כי חוש המשוש הוא חרפה לנו. חלילה, אין הדבר כמו שאמר היוני, לפי שדעתו היוני יש שמץ מינות שאינו מורגש, שאלו היה מאמין שהעולם מחודש בכוונה לא היה אומר כך זה היוני הבליעל.

אבל כל בעלי התורה מאמינים שהשם] (והשי"ת) ברא את הכל כפי מה שגזרה חכמתו, ולא ברא דבר שיהיה גנאי או כיעור, שאם יאמר שהחבור הוא דבר של גנאי, הנה כלי המשגל הם כלי הגנות,

2. Racanati, *Taamei Hamitzvot*: If it would be a bodily matter, it would not be called *yedia*, for *yedia* is the intention that something endures through *Hashem*'s providence.

who comes after the King? It has already been done." Midrash explains [*Kohelet Rabati*, 2:14] that *Hashem* and His Heavenly Court decided on each and every organ and established its function. If the sexual organs were shameful, how could *Hashem* have created them? If it were found that His actions are not perfect, the master of prophets [Moshe] would not proclaim [*Devarim* 32:4], "the *Tzur* [Creator, Rock], perfect are His actions," and [*Bereishit* 1:31] "*Elohim* saw all that He had made and behold! It was very good."

But the matter is as the prophet said [*Chabakuk* 1:13], that *Hashem* is "too pure to see evil"– there is no corruption or disgrace before Him, and He created man and woman and all their organs fashioned according to their function. The clear evidence is that Adam and Chava were naked, yet not ashamed [*Bereishit* 2:25]. Before the sin, they engaged in ideas, and all their intent was for the sake of Heaven, and to them, their sexual organs were like eyes or hands or any other organ. But when they deviated toward physical pleasure and did not intend their actions to be for the sake of Heaven by partaking of the fruit of the Tree of Knowledge, they knew they were naked [*Bereishit* 3:7]. When the hand writes a Torah scroll, it is honored, praiseworthy, and lofty, but when it steals, it is the opposite. Similarly, the sexual organs, when they do good, they are praiseworthy, but when they do evil, they are shameful and ugly. Thus, it occurs that the ways of *Hashem* are just, pure, and dignified. Whatever ugliness occurs is derived from the aspect of man's actions. Shlomo said [*Kohelet* 7:29], "God made man simple, but they have sought many intrigues," that is to say all human organs are perfect, having been created with supernal wisdom, but man's sin renders them impure and ugly.

Man's secret is wisdom [*chochma*] and woman's secret is understanding [*tevuna*] and their pure *chibur* [union, connection, act of intimacy] is the secret of *daat* [knowledge, awareness]. This is the secret of man and woman in the ways of Kabbala. *Chibur* is a most lofty matter when carried out properly.

והרי השי"ת בראם במאמרו דכתיב (דברים לב) הוא עשך ויכוננך ואז"ל במסכת חולין (נו ב) שברא הקב"ה כוננויות באדם. ובמדרש קהלת (ב, יב) אמרו אשר כבר עשוהו מלמד שהוא ובית דינו נמנו על כל אבר ואבר והושיבוהו על כנו. ואם כלי המשגל גנאי, היאך ברא הש"י דבר שיש בו משום חסרון או גנות חלילה, אלא פעולותיו של הקב"ה תמימות שנאמר (שם לב) הצור תמים פעלו. [ואומר וירא אלקים את כל אשר עשה והנה טוב מאד.]

אבל הענין הוא כמו שהש"י הוא טהור עינים מראות ברע (חבקוק א, יג) אין לפניו קלקול או גנאי והוא ברא איש ואשה וברא כל אבר ואבר שבהם והכינם על מתכונתם ולא ברא בהם דבר גנאי. והעדות הברורה מה שאמר במעשה בראשית (בראשית ב) ויהיו שניהם ערומים האדם ואשתו ולא יתבוששו, כל זה קודם שחטאו לפי שהיו עסוקין במושכלות וכל כונתם לשמים, ולא היו בעיניהם אלא כעינים ושאר אברי הגוף. אמנם כשנטו אחר ההנאות הגופניות ולא נתכוונו לשם שמים, אמר וידעו כי ערומים הם, ופי' כאשר הידים בעת שכותבין ס"ת בטהרה הם מכובדות ומשובחות וכשגונבות או עושות דבר מגונה הם מגונות, כך הם כלי המשגל לאדם ולאשתו קודם שחטאו. וכמו שיש בכל אבר ואבר מהאברים מהלל ושבח בעשות הטוב וגנאי בעשות הרע, כך היה לאדם הראשון בכלי המשגל. נמצא כי הקב"ה הוא כל דרכיו משפט וטהרה ונקיות, ונמצא הכעור כלו מצד פעולת האדם. על זה אמר שלמה המע"ה (קהלת ז) לבד ראה זה מצאתי אשר עשה האלקים את האדם ישר והמה בקשו חשבונות, כלומר אין בכל אברי האדם מצד הבריאה דבר קלקול או כיעור כי הכל בחכמה עליונית דבר מתוקן וטוב ונאה, אבל האדם בהיות סכל מביא כיעור בדברים שאין בהם כיעור מתחלה. והבן זה מאוד.

---

3. Rashi, *Yoma* 54b: The Cherubim embraced like a man and a woman. Some editions: The great secret of the *merkavot* [chariots, cherubs on the ark cover] which were attached to each other like man and woman in an intimate pose. If this would have been unseemly in any way, the Master of the Universe would not have commanded that it be made and put in the holiest and purest of places.

Guard carefully this secret – do not reveal it to anyone unworthy, the secret of Shlomo's Cherubim [*Melachim I*, 7:36].[3] When the Ammonites entered the Holy of Holies, they said, "Look who the gods of these people are!" and they shamed and blasphemed on account of the Cherubim [*Yoma* 54b]. If you would understand the secret of the Cherubim, and the Voice that was heard from between them,[4] you would know the saying of our rabbis, of blessed memory, that at the moment a man and his wife are intimate, the Divine Presence resides between them.

The name for man, *ish* contains a *yud*, and the name for woman, *Isha*, contains a *heh*, and when they unite in purity and holiness, they form a union of *yud heh*, the Unity of God. And when God is absent from between them, the result is *aish* and *aish*, fire and fire [Sota 17a].[5]

This was the secret the rabbis intended when they said [*Nidah* 31a] there are three partners in man – his father, his mother, and *Hashem* above. Furthermore, they said [*Pesachim* 30b] when a person honors his mother and father, *Hashem* says He considers it as though He dwells between them and He Himself is honored. If this intimate embrace is shameful in any way, how can He be found there? *Hashem* is involved in the mating /conception process as we see from Avraham, whom He told [*Bereishit* 17:16], "I will bless her, and I have given to you from her a son." With Rivka [*Bereishit* 25:21], "*Hashem* let Himself be entreated by him, and Rivka, his wife conceived." With Leah and Rachel [*Bereishit* 29:31 and 30:22], "and He opened her womb" and with Chana [*Shmuel I* 1:9], "And Elkana knew his wife Chana…and *Hashem* remembered her." Torah tells us [*Shemot* 23:27], "There will not be miscarriage and barrenness in your land" and the rabbis said [*Taanit* 2a] "Three keys were not given to any intermediary" and one of them is conception. If this would be in any way deprecatory, why is *Hashem* Himself taking care of it?

When Yehuda turns toward Tamar [*Bereishit* 39:17], the midrash notes [*Bereishit Rabba* ad loc.] that Yehuda wanted to

והנה סוד הידיעה שאני רומז לך הוא סוד היות האדם כלול בסוד חכמה ותבונה ודעת, כי האדם הוא סוד החכמה והאשה סוד התבונה והחבור הטהור הוא סוד הדעת. וזהו סוד איש ואשה בסוד דרכי הקבלה הפנימית. וא"כ ענין החבור הזה ענין עילוי גדול כשיהיה כפי הראוי.

והסוד הגדול הזה סוד גדול בכרובים שהיו מעורים זה בזה דמיון זכר ונקבה. ואילו היה הדבר גנאי לא היה מצוה רבונו של עולם לעשות ככה ולשום אותם במקום היותר קדוש וטהור שבכל הישוב, אלא שהוא על סוד עמוק מאד. ושמור הסוד הזה ואל תגלהו לשום אדם אלא אם כן הוא הגון וראוי לו, כי מכאן נראה סוד עלוי החבור הראוי.

וזהו סוד בנין שלמה שכתוב (מכלים א, ז, לו) כמער איש ולויות, איש המעורה בלויות שלו, ועל זה אמר דוד המלך ע"ה (תהלים סט, כא) חרפה שברה לבי ואנושה, אמרו רז"ל (מדרש איכא פתיחתא ט) כשהרגישו עמונים ואמרו ראו אלהיהם של אלו עושה כזו וחירפו וגידפו בענין הכרובים. ואם תבין סוד הכרובים ממה שנאמר והקול נשמע מביניהם.

תדע מה שאמרו חז"ל בשעה שאדם מתחבר עם אשתו בקדושה ובטהרה שכינה שרויה ביניהם. נתחממו שכינה מסתלקת מביניהם וישאר אש ואש. כדגרסינן בסוטה (יז א) היה דורש ר"ע איש ואשה זכו שכינה ביניהם, לא זכו אש אוכלתם. פי' כשהאדם מתחבר לאשתו בקדושה שכינה ביניהם, תמצא בשם האיש יו"ד ובשם האשה ה' הרי זה שמו של הקב"ה מצוי ביניהם. אבל אם לא נתכוונו לחבור קדושה אלא למלאות תאותם ומתוך התאוה והחמוד נתחממו כאש, יו"ד של שם

4. *Yishayahu* 37:16: Lord Almighty, G-d of Israel enthroned between the Cherubim. You alone are G-d over all the kingdoms of the earth. You have made heaven and earth. *Bamidbar* 7:89: When Moshe entered the Tent of Meeting to speak with *Hashem*, he heard the Voice speaking to him between the two Cherubim above the *kaporet* which is upon the Ark of the Testimony from between the two Cherubim, and He spoke to him.

5. *Bereishit* 1:20: He did not find a helpmate *knegdo* [opposing him, corresponding to him]. Sota 17a: Rabbi Akiva explained: If they merit it [by virtue of the intent of their intimate act], the Divine Presence is between them. If they do not merit this, a fire consumes them.

pass her by. *Hashem* prepared an angel designated for desire to inform him of *Hashem*'s intent and wish for his *chibur* with her. As a result of the intent of the two of them to fulfill *Hashem*'s will, twins were born, both righteous, both pure, comparable to the sun and moon – Peretz and Zarach. When righteous people unite, it is said of the product of their *chibur* [*Yirmiyahu* 1:4], "Before I formed you in the womb, I knew you."[6]

If so, the words of the Greek scoundrel [Aristotle] are invalid. When the union of the couple is done in Heaven's Name, there is nothing more holy and pure. Therefore, it is said of the righteous couple, "Before I formed you in the womb I knew you" [*Yirmiyahu* 1], relating to Hashem's formation of the righteous person from the drop of seed. But in the case of an evil person, that drop breaks forth in impurity and Hashem, may He be blessed, has no portion in it, upon which is written, "evil ones are estranged from the womb" [*Tehilim* 58].

The proper union of a man and his wife is comparable to the Creation of heaven and earth, as the prophet declares [*Zecharya* 12:1], "Thus says the Lord of Hosts, Who inclines the heavens and founds the earth and creates the spirit of man inside him." Furthermore, [*Amos* 9:6] "He founds His group upon the earth," meaning He and the parents constitute a group for the purpose of creating man. That is the secret of [*Bereishit* 1:26] "Let us make man in Our image." This partnership results from the mother and father contributing the bodily order[7] and *Hashem* casting into it the soul, as the Torah says [*Bereishit* 2:7], "And He blew into his nostrils the living soul." The reversal of this creative process is described by Shlomo [*Kohelet* 12:7], "And He will return the dust to the earth as it had been, and the spirit will return to the God who gave it." If *Hashem* Himself, in His Glory and His Essence, participates in human conception, it is clear that *chibur* of man and wife is proper and pure, the secret of the building of the world.

Now that I have awakened you to one way of one kind of intimacy, I will enlighten and inform you of the second kind,

האיש וה' של שם האשה שהוא י"ה מסתלק מביניהם ונשאר אש ואש. [והבן זה כי בכאן יש כל הסוד.]

ואל זה הסוד נתכוונו ז"ל באמרם (נדה לא א) ג' שותפין יש בו באדם, ואלו הן איש ואשה והקב"ה [ואמרו בגמ' קידושין (ל ב) בזמן שאדם מכבד את אביו ואמו הקב"ה אומר מעלה אני עליהם כאילו דרתי ביניהם וכבדוני.] ואם היה הדבר גנאי היאך היו כוללים את השי"ת בדבר שהוא כך. והנה השי"ת אמר לאברהם בענין מולד יצחק (בראשית יז) וברכתי אותה וגם נתתי ממנה לך בן, ובענין רבקה (שם כה) ויעתר יצחק לה' לנכח אשתו, ובענין רחל ולאה (שם כט) ויפתח את רחמה, ובענין אלקנה (ש"א א' יט) וידע אלקנה את חנה אשתו ויזכרה ה'. והנה בכלל הברכות (שמות כג) לא תהיה משכלה ועקרה. ועוד גרסינן בתענית (ב א, ב ב) שלש מפתחות לא נמסרו ביד שליח ואחד מהן ההריון שנאמר ויפתח את רחמה וגו'. ואלו היה בדבר גנאי, מה לו להקב"ה לעשותו בלי שליח.

ובב"ר (פ"ה ח) בענין (בראשית לח) ויט אליה אל הדרך, בקש יהודה לעבור, רמז הקב"ה למלאך הממונה על התאוה. ובא להודיע כי כוונת הש"י וחפצו היתה בחבור זה. ולפיכך נולדו שניהם תאומים שניהם צדיקים שניהם טהורים, כדוגמת שמש וירח, פרץ וזרח. והבן כי כצורת סדרי עולם נולדו, ואין בחבור שלהם גנאי כאשר אין גנאי בתיקון סדרי עולם כללם ופרטם. ובענין רות נאמר (רות ד) ויתן ה' לה הריון וגו', ואלו היה בדבר גנות הרי כבר נאמר (חבקוק א') והבט אל עמל לא אוכל, וכתיב שם: טהור עינים מראות ברע.

[וא"כ נמצאו דברי היוני הבליעל הבלים בטלים מצד אחד. והוא] כשיהיה החבור לשם שמים אין דבר קדוש ונקי למעלה הימנו. ולפיכך נאמר בחבור הצדיקים (ירמיה א) בטרם אצרך בבטן ידעתיך, הנה ייחס

---

6. *Melachim I* 7:36: The Cherubim… embraced each other like a man and his mate. Recanati, *Bereishit* 11:2: From here you understand the secret of *zivug* [coupling]. Know and understand this matter that all existence is based on the model of the embrace of man and his mate. The relationship of the Upper World to its shadow the Lower world, is like that, as our rabbis of blessed memory said in the *Book of Bahir* [clarity].

7. Think homunculus, or better, DNA.

the opposite of the first. When a person does not intend it for the Name of Heaven, that seed is a putrid drop that *Hashem* has no part in, called [*Bereishit* 38:9] the corruption of man's way on earth, the planting of *ashera* [tree of idolatry], fattening of calves for strange worship, in that it is the planting of corrupted seed. The resultant offspring are evildoers foreign from the womb. Therefore, *Hashem* tells us [*Vayikra* 20:26] "Be holy for I am holy."

MDK: The author cites the offensive Rambam text in the Guide, and instead of attacking the Torah giant, he attacks his mentor, the Greek. This quote may have been the source of the beloved student's distress. Rambam was apparently impressed with Greek wisdom and Greek medicine and sought to synthesize contemporary wisdom with Torah. The author proves from scriptural and rabbinic sources his error in seeing disgrace in intimacy. The most impressive proof of the holiness of intimacy is the Cherubim in the holiest place in the holy of holies where the Shechina resides. They are depicted as embracing like a man and a woman. Chibur is the essence of holiness.

צורת הצדיק אל הבורא ית' כאילו הוא מצייר טפת הזרע הנמשכת מן הצדיק, ואמר בטרם אצרך בבטן. אבל ברשע הפריץ אותה הטפה כולה טמאה אין לשם ית' חלק בה, ועליה נאמר (תהלים נח) זורו רשעים מרחם. [הבן זה, שהם זרים ונכרים ואינם חלק הש"י.]

[והנה כל הדברים שאמרנו הם בסוד מערכת סדרי עולם ובנינו ודוגמת זכרים ונקבות בסוד משפיע ומקבל השפע.] והנה חבור האדם אל אשתו כראוי פי' ז"ל שהיא כדמיון שמים וארץ שנאמר (זכריה יב) נאם ה' נוטה שמים ויוסד ארץ ויוצר רוח אדם בקרבו, ואומר (עמוס ט) ואגודתו על ארץ יסדה, והם אגודה אחת לברוא אדם וזה [סוד] נעשה אדם בצלמנו, כלומר גם אני שותף בבריאת האדם, והשותפות הזו, כי מן האב והאם נמשכין כל סדרי הגוף והש"י זורק בו נשמה, כאמרו (בראשית ב) ויפח באפיו נשמת חיים, ואומרו (קהלת יב) וישוב העפר על הארץ כשהיה והרוח תשוב אל אלקים אשר נתנה [לכן אתם בעלי עיניים, ראו אם יש גנות בדבר שהש"י שותף בו. אם כן נמצא חבור האדם לאשתו כשהוא כראוי שהוא סוד בנין העולם וישובו, כי האדם נעשה שותף להקב"ה במעשה בראשית.]

[והנה סוד זה שאמרנו בזמן שהאדם מתחבר לאשתו בקדושה ובטהרה שכינה ביניהם בסוד איש ואשה, וזה הוא סוד בטרם אצרך בבטן ידעתיך וסוד קדש לי כל בכור פטר כל רחם, ומה שאמרו נתחממו שכינה מסתלקת מביניהם בסוד אש ואש והוא סוד זורו רשעים מרחם, והבן זה מאד.]

ואחר שהודענוך על סוד הדרך האחד מן החבור, נודיעך הדרך השני והוא הפך הראשון, כי בזמן שאין אדם מתכוין לשם שמים הנה אותו הזרע הנמשך היא טפה סרוחה, אין לשם ית' חלק בה, ונקרא משחית דרכו על הארץ, והנה גופו כלה לבהלה, וכאילו נוטע אשרה ומפטם עגלים לע"א, בהיותו זרע מקולקל וטפה שלא נזרקה בה נשמה רק כסלון ממאיר ועליו נאמר (תהלים נח) זורו רשעים מרחם. והנה צוה הקב"ה בתורה ואמר והייתם לי קדושים כי קדוש אני. [ועוד אבאר זה בפרקים הבאים.]

Chapter Three

The Timing of the Intimate Act

HASHEM, MAY HE be blessed, said in the Torah with respect to marital obligations [*Shemot* 21:10], "He shall not diminish her food, her clothing, or her *ona* [consortium, satisfaction of her sexual needs]. The latter is defined in the Talmud [*Ketuvot* 61b] according to occupation [sailor once in three months, camel driver once a month, Torah scholar every Shabbat eve]. When the psalmist says "It will give forth its fruit in its time" [*Tehilim* 1:3] – this is the *ona* of a Torah scholar.

It is known that a man's seed is actually his bodily life force and the luminescence of his shine, for it is the clarified and purified blood: otherwise, the *tzura* [spiritual essence] would not be imprinted there. The seed is itself a part of the body, yet it has potential portions[8] of every organ, for it is known that an eye cannot give rise to an ear and vice versa, for organs give rise to like organs, just as wheat does not reproduce as beans, and a donkey does not reproduce as a sheep or an ox. Each organ and tissue has a specific nature and a specific precursor from which it develops in the seed. Such a complex vital bodily part of a man should not be continually spent inside his wife as is the case with roosters, for then his power would weaken and the illumination of his eyes would diminish, and all his bodily parts would deteriorate.

הנה הש"י אמר בתורה (שמות כא) שארה כסותה ועונתה לא יגרע. ועונה האמורה בתורה מפורשת בגמרא (כתובות סא ב) כי העונות משתנות כפי סדר כל בני אדם. ועכשיו נניח לדבר בעונת שאר בני אדם ונדבר בעונת ת"ח הראוי, שהוא מלילי שבת ללילי שבת. ועל זה אמרו (כתובות סב ב) אשר פריו יתן בעתו גו׳, זו היא עונת ת"ח.

ודע כי זרע האדם הוא חיי גופו ומאור זהרו כי הוא הדם המובחר והזך אשר בגוף, שאילו לא היה כן לא היתה צורת אדם בו. הנה הזרע הוא מחלקי הגוף ויש לו חלק מכל אבר ואבר, כי בידוע שלא יולד אזן מעין ולא עין מאזן, רק כל אבר נמשך מטבע אבר דומה לו, כמו שלא יצמח מזרע החטה פולין ועדשים לא מזרע אדם חמור או שור או שה. וכל אבר ואבר וכל צורה וצורה יש לו טבע מיוחד וכח ידוע שממנו נולד, ואין לחוש לסומא שמוליד פקח כי כח האבר מצוי בטבע הכללי שבגוף וא"כ הזרע הוא חלק מכל אבר ואבר מאברי הגוף. ולכן אין ראוי לאדם להיות מצוי אצל אשתו כתרנגול כי אז היה כחו תשש ומאור עיניו מתמעט וכל חלקי איבריו הולכים ודלים.

8. Think molecular precursors.

But if his intimate activity is carried out at known specific intervals, like Sabbath night to Sabbath night, he will be able to provide energy beyond himself, and lack nothing, for during the seven-day interval he has been energized. This is what the Psalmist means "giving forth fruit in its proper time," from Sabbath night to Sabbath night, "and its leaves shall not wither," his heavenly intentioned intimate act will successfully be concluded [Gemara], "and everything he does will succeed" [*Tehilim* 1:3].

Why Sabbath night? Sabbath is the Secret of the World, a model of the World of Souls, and the rabbis intended the *ona* of Torah scholars to occur on Sabbath, that their direction be toward the spiritual soul, to conceive a *tzura*[9] fitting to serve *Hashem*, possessor of a pure and lofty spiritual soul. Torah tells us [*Shemot* 31:17], "And on the seventh day He ceased work and rested [*vayinafash*]" refers to the *ona* of Torah scholars. The fitting time for this is not the work days, which are body-related, but rather the day of Sabbath and restfulness, the World of Souls.

Once you have been awakened to this, we can return to what we intended to clarify – the three aspects of the timing of *chibur*. The first is day, which has been discussed. The second is the temporal relationship between *chibur* and eating, and the third is the proper hour.

After a person eats, there are three stages of digestion, then in the fourth stage the food is converted to either white blood [chyle] that sustains the body, or semen, and if a person engages in intercourse too soon after eating, his blood is not clear and pure, and his nature is heated. At that moment, the semen extracted from this blood is corrupted, spoiled and unclean, and the offspring that is founded from that seed is likewise corrupted and unclean; about which it is said [*Tehilim* 7:16], "He conceives mischief and brings forth falsehood" and [*Tehilim* 58:4] "Evildoers are foreign from the womb." Therefore, a person must direct the timing of intimacy to be a time when he is comfortable with himself [*nafsho myushevet alav*], and the

אבל בהיות החבור בעונה הידועה שהיא מליל שבת לליל שבת, שהוא סוד החזרת הגלגלים פנים ואחור בשבעת ימי השבוע, אז יוכל להשפיע כח בזולתו והוא לא יחסר דבר שיהיה נחלש (עליו) [ממנו] חולשת נראית, לפי שכבר קבל כח שיוכל להשפיע ממנו. ולפיכך אמר (תהלים א, ג) אשר פריו יתן בעתו, והיינו מליל שבת לליל שבת. וסמיך ליה ועלהו לא יבול, כלומר והיה החבור לשם שמים ויבא לידי גמר מעשה.

וטעם היותו מליל שבת לליל שבת, לפי שהשבת הוא יסוד עולם והוא דוגמת עולם הנפשות מטעם שבת לה׳. וכוונו חכמים בעונת ת״ח מליל שבת לליל שבת [כונתם לנפש השכלית] להוליד צורה הראויה לעבודת הבורא יתברך בעלת נשמה שכלית עליונה וטהורה כאמרו (שמות לא) וביום השביעי שבת וינפש. והנה זאת הכונה בעונת ת״ח. והבן מאד, כי לא שמו עונתן בימי הגופנים דהיינו ששת ימי המעשה כי אם ביום שכולו שבת ועולם הנפשות. [והבן וייטב לך. כדאיתא בספר ר׳ נחוניא בן הקנה (ע׳ ב״ר פ׳ יא) שבת קרא תגר לפני הש״י רבונו של עולם לכל נתת זוג ולי לא נתת זוג. אמר ליה בתי כנסת ישראל תהיה זוגך.]

ואחר אשר עוררנוך על זה, נחזור למה שהיתה כוונתנו [לבארו] (לסדרו), ונאמר כי זמן החבור נחלק לג׳ חלקים, החלק הא׳ זמן עונה בימים. החלק השני, זמן עונה מצד המזון. החלק הג׳, זמן עונה מצד השעות. אמנם החלק הא׳ כבר בארנוהו בפרק זה. והחלק השני מן הג׳ חלקים שהוא זמן העונה מצד המזון תצטרך לדעת בעז״ה.

ודע כי המזון שאדם נזון בו צריך שלשה מיני שנויים ולמדרגה הד׳ נהפך לזרע או לדם לבן מפרנס את הגוף. ואילו ישמש האדם מטתו סמוך לאכילה, הנה באותו זמן טבע הגוף רותח והדם עכור מעורב ואינו זך וצלול, והנה אותה הטפה הנמשכת מעליו עכורה ומלוכלכת, סרוחה ומטונפת, אינה נקיה ולא טהורה. ונמצא הולד מאותה טפה מיסוד עכור ומטונף, עליו נאמר (תהלים ז) הרה עמל וילד שקר, ואומר (שם נח) זורו רשעים מרחם, לפי שמטבע מזג הטפה שאינה זכה מחייב להיות

9. *Tzura*, form, is a metaphor for spirituality, and its opposite, chomer, material, is a metaphor for physicality.

bodily nature is quieted down from the roiling of the food he ate, and the blood is cleared, and the sediment has settled to its natural place, and the fundaments of the body are in proper order, which is approximately after midnight.

In the Talmud [*Berachot* 5b], Abba Binyamin says, "I worried all my life…that my bed be oriented north/ south." And Rabbi Yitzchak said if one's bed is oriented north/south, one will have male children, as it is written [*Tehilim* 17:14], "With *tzafoncha* [your hidden treasure, north] you fill their belly, they are sated with sons." Rav Nachman bar Yitzchak said one's wife will not suffer a miscarriage, as "fill" occurs in this verse, and the Torah says, "her days were filled to give birth." I must tell you what this is about. No fool in the world would think that the orientation of a bed can influence having sons or not having miscarriages, ever more so these great rabbis, pillars of the world. They are hiding their words in hints as is their custom.

It is well known that strong cold comes from the north and great heat from the south, and such extremes are not good and proper, rather the moderate characteristics are the choice ones. On this King Shlomo said [*Kohelet* 7:16], "Be not too righteous or too wise." Here the sages are saying, when it comes to intimate relations, do not be too hot or too cold, but have your bodily temperament in between, so as to have one's nature in a comfortable state and not lose control over one's seed, so that she heats up and "gives seed" first. Then her seed is the material on which his seed gives form. This is the secret behind [*Vayikra* 12:2] "If a woman gives seed and has a male child," on which the sages said [*Nidah* 71a] that on account of the righteous waiting at the womb, they are rewarded with male offspring, as King David said [*Tehilim* 127:3], "Behold *Hashem*'s inheritance – sons, a reward of the fruit of the womb." To understand this is to understand the underlying meaning of the north/south orientation of the bed and its relation to male children.

Midnight is the time of quiet following the heating up of nature by the food, and the condition of the body is pure and

הנוצר ממנה משוקץ ומטונף. לפיכך צריך האדם לכוין שעת החבור בשעה שנפשו מיושבת עליו ושקט טבע הגוף מרתיחת המזון שאכל ונזדקק הדם וירדו השמרים למקומם הטבעי, ואז יסודות גוף האדם יהיו מסודרות בסדר נכון שהוא סמוך לחצי הלילה האחרון.

ועל זה אז"ל במסכת ברכות (ה ב) אבא בנימין אומר כל ימי הייתי מצטער על שני דברים על מטתי שתהא נתונה בין צפון לדרום וכו', ואמרי ר' יצחק הנותן מטתו בין צפון לדרום הויין לו בנים זכרים שנאמר (שם יז) וצפונך תמלא בטנם ישבעו בנים והניחו יתרם לעולליהם. רב נחמן בר יצחק אמר אף אשתו אינה מפלת נפלים, כתיב הכא תמצא בטנם וכתיב התם (בראשית כה) וימלאו ימיה ללדת וגו'. וצריך אני לעורר על המדה הזו, ידוע שאין פתי או סכל בעולם סובר כי מפני נתינת המטה בין צפון לדרום זוכה אדם להיות לו בנים זכרים ושלא תהא אשתו מפלת נפלים, כ"ש שיאמרו עמודי עולם אנשים חכמים ונבונים כאלו הדברים. אמנם כי הם דברו הדברים נרמזים כמנהגם הטוב בכל מקום. והנני מבאר.

ידוע כי הקור החזק הוא לפאת צפון והחום החזק לפאת דרום. וחכמי האמת יודעים כי הרחקת האדם אל הקצוות אינו מדין הטוב והישר, אבל המדות הבינוניות הם המובחרות. ועל זה אמר שלמה ע"ה (קהלת ז) אל תהי צדיק הרבה ואל תתחכם יותר אל תרשע הרבה ואל תהי סכל. לפי שצפון ודרום הם שני הפכים לחום ולקור, הסתירו רבותנו ז"ל דבריהם ורמזום, ואמרו כי המשמש מטתו בהיות מזג גופו ממוצע בין החום ובין הקור אז יוכלו טבעיו לנוח ולא יזריע מהרה, אבל יוכל לבעול במתון, ואז האשה מקדמת להזריע תחלה, ונמצא זרע האשה כדמיון החומר, וכי יבא אחר כך זרע האיש נמצא כדמיון היוצר שמצייר צורה בחומר, וזהו סוד אשה כי תזריע שילדה זכר וזהו סוד שארז"ל (נדה לא) בשכר שמשהין הצדיקים על בטן האשה הויין להו בנים זכרים שנאמר (תהלים קכז) הנה נחלת ה' בנים שכר פרי הבטן. ובהיותך מבין כל זה, תבין סוד הנותן מטתו בין צפון לדרום הויין לו בנים זכרים.

נמצא זה בחצי הלילה שכבר שקט הגוף מרתיחת טבע המזון שאכל ומזג הגוף צח ונקי. ומה שאמרו חז"ל בין צפון לדרום, רצה לומר בין הקור לחום. ידוע כי כל איש שנולד מטפה קרה יהיה לעולם פתי וסכל [ומשולח] ומי שנולד מטפה חמה יהיה בעל חמה וכעס [ונקלה], אבל

cleansed. It is known that a person conceived from a cold drop will be foolish and lack intelligence, and a person conceived from a hot drop will be hot-tempered and easy to anger. But a person conceived from a drop intermediate between hot and cold will always be wise and understanding, of calm temperament, and socially involved.

What is the connection between miscarriage and the north/south orientation of the bed? Rabbi Chanina said [*Yoma* 82b] of the fetus that whispered demands to its mother on Yom Kippur [*Tehilim* 58:4], "evildoers are foreign from the womb,"[10] He understood the "evil" fetus was in danger of being expelled from the womb because he suffered an extreme lack of a certain nutrient, and he saved it from miscarriage by allowing the mother to accede to the unremitting demand of the fetus for the forbidden food. It is known that the cause of miscarriage is the provocation of the womb by the extremes of hunger and satiation – heat and cold. When the womb is in moderation, miscarriage does not occur. The orientation of the bed is a metaphor for the proper timing of intimacy, so as to create a moderate temperament in the resultant fetus.

We have included in chapter three aspects of the timing of intimate relations, the day, the food, and the hour.

MDK: The author metaphorically employs the reproductive physiology that our blessed rabbis learned from the wisdom of the Greeks of their time. Raban Gamliel even ran a school to prepare representatives of our people to communicate with their contemporaries in the non-Jewish world. These biological references serve to teach us spiritual principles to steer us through the treacherous straits of intimacy.

Reproduction aside, the goal of sexual intimacy is the mitzvah of ona, the sexual gratification of the woman. The happiness of the man is the fulfillment of this mitzvah. Nowhere in The Holy Letter will you see any mention of man's pleasure.

הנולד מטפה ממוצעת בין החום והקור יהיה לעולם חכם יקר רוח איש תבונה ויהיה בדעותיו מעורב עם הבריות, ועל זה נאמר (שמואל א' א') ונתתה לאמתך זרע אנשים, ומה שדרשו ז"ל בגמרא ברכות (לא ב) לא אוכם ולא חוור לא טפש ולא ארוך ולא גוץ, כי כל אלו המדות הווֹת באדם בהיות מזגו בין קור לחום, שזהו סוד בין צפון לדרום וזהו סוד בנים זכרים שאמרנו.

אבל מה שאמרו אין אשתו מפלת נפלים, יש בענין זה עיקר גמור. והנני פותח לך שערי אורה. בזה כבר ידעת מה שאז"ל (יומא פב ב) בענין ההיא עוברה שהריחה ביוה"כ לחישו לה ולחיש, שזהו בין צפון לדרום, קרא עליה (ירמיה א) בטרם אצרך בבטן ידעתיך וההיא עוברה דלחישו לה ולא לחיש, שזה נוטה לפאת דרום, קרא עליה (תהלים נח) זורו רשעים מרחם. וידוע כי סבת המפלת נפלים היא בהתעורר הרחם לאחד הקצוות, אם לרעב אם לתאוה מפלת, אם לחום אם לקור. כי בהיות הרחם ממוצע לעולם לא תפיל, כאשר הפלס בעין משפט שלא יטו המאזנים לאחת הצדדין, ואם כן הלחישו לה ולא לחיש נוטה מן הקצה האמצעי והוא קרוב להיות נפל אם לא יאכילהו מדבר שהריח. ואם תאמר הנה גם אם הצדיק הריחה. אף על פי שהריחה הנה חזרה לפלס האמצעי, [אבל אם הוא רשע שהריחה לא חזרה לפלס האמצעי, אמנם נטתה לקצה הבהמיות שבה ולא יכלה להתאפק בקצה האמצעי].

א"כ בין והתבונן בזמן שראוי לו לאדם לשמש ותזכה לבנים ראוים להוראה. והנה כללנו (בדרך) [בפרק] הזה ג' זמנים לעונה, מצד הימים ומצד המזון ומצד השעות.

10. *Yoma* 82b discusses a case of a pregnant woman with an irresistible urge to eat on Yom Kippur, her fetus having sensed or smelled a certain food. Rabbi Chanina whispered in her ear (for the fetus) that that day was Yom Kippur, but the lust of the fetus continued, whereupon Rabbi Chanina recited the verse (*Tehilim* 58:4], "Evildoers are foreign from the womb." The fetus grew up to be Shabtai the fruit warehouser, whose manipulative speculations drove up the price of fruit and made it unavailable to the people.

Chapter Four

Food and the Intimate Act

All of *Hashem*'s ways are just, yet He commanded us to slaughter animals for food. Why did He do this? We could have been sustained with fruits, vegetables, and grain. Why abandon the blood of animals to their great pain? Understand that the world is founded on the principle that *Hashem*, may He be blessed, acts for the benefit of all His creatures and is merciful to all His creatures, and on this King David said [*Tehilim* 145:9], "*Hashem* is good to all, and His mercy is upon all that He made." This verse tells us that killing and eating animals by people is a benefit for the animals and a mercy for them, as I will explain.

It is known that the food man eats is ground up in the stomach and descends to the small intestine. From there, the liver sucks the good, choice, fatty, pure, and clean elements of the food and pushes the remainder to the large intestine, from whence it emerges as excrement. The good food elements are processed and cleansed by the liver and converted to blood, which is sent to the heart, whence it is further sent to the organs. There, the end organ processes it further – muscle makes muscle, fat makes fat, bone makes bone, blood vessels make blood vessels, and this is how the whole body is nourished. Thus, an animal killed for human consumption and then eaten rises in status from animal to human.

הדרך השלישי - המזון הראוי לחבור

והנה הש"י שכל דרכיו משפט צוה לשחוט בהמות למאכלנו, ומה לו לזה והלא טוב להיותנו נזונים במיני פירות ומגדים, ומה לו להפקיר דם בהמות וחיות ולצערם צער גדול. דע כי אלו הם מוסדות עולם שהש"י מטיב לכל בריה והוא מרחם על בריותיו. ועל זה נאמר (תהלים קמה) טוב י"י לכל ורחמיו על כל מעשיו. הודיע בפסוק זה כי שחיטת בעלי חיים ואכילתן על ידי בני אדם לטובת בעלי חיים היא, וחמלה ורחמים עליהם. והנני מבאר.

ידוע כי כל מזון שאדם אוכל הוא הולך באסטומכא, ומשם יורד למעים העליונים, ומשם הכבד מוצץ הטוב והמובחר והשמן והזך והנקי שבאותו מזון, והשאר דוחה אותו למעים האחרונים ויוצא דרך הרעי. ואותו הדבר שהכבד מוצץ, חוזר ומבשלו ומחזירו דם, ומנקה אותו ומשלחו ללב, והלב משלחו לכל האברים, וחוזר בכל אבר ואבר ממין האבר בבישול שלישי, וחוזר בבשר בשר, ובשומן שומן, ובגידים גידים, ובעצמות עצמות, כי ממנו הגוף נזון. ואם כן נמצאת בהמה זו שנשחטה, לטובתה נשחטה, שעלתה ממדרגת גוף בהמה למדרגת גוף אדם.

וזהו דרך ד' הרכבות עולם התחתון, שהן מקורות וצמחים ובעלי חיים שאינם מדברים ובעלי חיים המדברים, כי המקורות שואבין וניזונין מד' יסודות, והצמחים ניזונים מד' יסודות ומן המקורות, ובעלי

There are four classes of substance in our lower world – non-life entities, plants, animals who do not speak, and man, who speaks. Non-living creations are nourished by the four elements – water, earth, wind, and fire; plants from the same four plus the nonliving creations; animals from the previous five plus the plants; and living speaking beings from the previous six plus animals. Each level makes an ascent to a higher level by providing it with nourishment.

Consider that blood nourishes body and turns into body. Blood takes on the nature of that which it is made. When food is thick and murky, the blood it makes is thick and murky. And when it is clear and clean, the blood it makes is similarly clear, clean, and pure. *Hashem* separated us in His holy Torah from various forbidden foods. Some of them stop up the heart, like forbidden fats and blood. Some of them cause arrogance, like predatory beasts and birds, some break up the parts of understanding, like rabbits, coneys, and pigs, some cause harsh diseases, like swarming water and land creatures. In summary, scripture says [*Vayikra* 20:25] of all of these, "Do not abominate your souls with forbidden animals and birds and all the creepers of the earth from which I have separated you." He has made it known that these things thicken and make loathsome and give rise to bad blood, capable of producing all types of calamities.

If so, when the sages say to sanctify one's self at the time of intimacy, the food one eats is part of that sanctification – proper, moderate food, not too hot, not too cold, foods that give rise to pure, clean blood, destined to be converted to semen, which is further destined to be the foundation and the building of the fetus resulting from that intimate act. If the food is right, the semen will be clean and moderate, and if the food is thick and turbid, so will be the semen. It follows that the food is a cause of the resultant child being wise or foolish, righteous or evil.

As we say, the Holy One, blessed be He, approximated the portion of the woman who gives seed in our Torah to the portion of forbidden foods. The verse [*Vayikra* 11:47] "To distinguish

חיים שאינן מדברים נזונים מן הצמחים והמקורות ומד׳ יסודות, והחי המדבר משתמש מן החיים שאינן מדברים ומן הצמחים ומן המקורות ומד׳ יסודות. וכן כל דבר הולך מעלוי לעלוי עד שהגלגל חוזר פנים ואחור, ועל זה נאמר טוב י״י לכל, מן היסודות עולה למדרגה למעלה מהן והן המקורות, והמקורות עולות למדרגה למעלה מהן והם הצמחים הצומחים, ומן הצמחים עולין למעלה מהן והם בעלי חיים שאינם מדברים שמתנועעים וצומחים והם מורכבים מד׳ יסודות, ומבעלי חיים שאין מדברים עולים למעלה גדולה מהם והם החיים המדברים שיש בהם כח דיבור וכח תנועה וכח צמיחה וכח הרכבה מד׳ יסודות. אם כן נמצאו כל הדברים נעשין מזון לזולתם כדי לעלותם לעילוי גדול על מדרגתם.

ואחר הקדמה זו, דע שבהיות הדם מזון הגוף ונהפך לגוף, והדם הוא כפי טבע המזון שנעשה ממנו, ראוי לך לדעת כי בהיות המזון עב ועכור יהיה הדם הנעשה ממנו עב ועכור, ואם המזון הוא נקי זך וטהור יהיה הדם כמותו. ולפיכך הבדילנו יתברך בתורתו הקדושה מכמה מאכלות אסורות שאסר אותם עלינו, קצתם מטמטמין את הלב כחלב ודם, וקצתם שמעזין את הפנים כחיות ועופות ובהמות הדורסין, וקצתם שסוגרין דלתי התבונה והחכמה כארנבת ושפן וחזיר ודומיהן, וקצתן שמולידין כמה מיני חלאים קשים ורעים כשרצי הארץ והמים. סוף דבר על כלם אמר (ויקרא יא) אל תשקצו את נפשותיכם, הרי הודיע כי כל אלו הדברים נתעבים ונמאסים ועושין דם רע מוכן לכמה פורעניות.

והנה אם כן כשאמרו (נדה עא א) שצריך אדם לקדש עצמו בשעת תשמיש, הנה גם המזון כלול בקדוש הזה כי ראוי לאדם לאכול מזונות ראוים והגונים ממוצעים בין הקור והחום, ויהיו מן הדברים המולידים דם נקי וזך וטהור מאחר שאותו הדם עתיד להיות נהפך לטפת הזרע והוא עתיד להיות יסוד ובנין לולד הנולד מאותו חבור, כי אלו היה המזון רע ועכור ועב תהיה גם הטפה עבה מטונפת ועכורה. ואם כן נמצא המזון [הנלקח טרם החבור הוא סבה] (להוויית האדם הכנה) להיות [הולד] חכם או פתי או צדיק או רשע.

והנני מוסר בידך מפתח גדול. דע כי בהיות הדבר כמו שאנו אומרים, סמך השם יתברך בתורתו הקדושה פרשת אשה כי תזריע למאכלות אסורות ואמר (ויקרא יא) ולהבדיל בין הטמא ובין הטהור ובין החיה

between pure and impure, and animals that may be eaten from animals not to be eaten" is immediately followed by [*Vayikra* 12:2] "If a woman gives seed" which is then followed by the portion of *metzora* [a disease of impurity]. These three portions imply a remarkable secret – if one separates one's self from forbidden foods, one will have proper, pure holy children, and if not, powerful and great plagues will arise from the seed that originated in the forbidden food.

This comes to inform you that man needs to sanctify himself with proper food near the time of conjugal relations, in order that the resultant offspring be from clean, pure, moderate seed, between North and South as we have explained. According to the food eaten will be the blood of the parent, and according to the blood will be the seed, and according to the seed the offspring will be born. You know already that a horse cannot bear an eagle, and wheat cannot come from beans. Likewise, it is said that the result of a bad, murky seed can be only ugly and abominable, as King David said, "The wicked are estranged from the womb" [*Tehilim* 58].

I have informed you of proper food. It must also be taken in a moderate quantity, to allow for natural digestion to quickly change to blood that is clean and pure, for if there is excessive food in the stomach, even proper food, it will not be properly digested and will revert to bad, coarse, and evil. Quantity as well as quality must be paid attention to. Guard this essential matter with regard to preparing for marital relations.

MDK: The physiologic metaphors continue into this chapter which deals with nutrition and digestion. Here also, holiness extends and Torah rules apply to set the bounds of eating options. The bridge to reproductive activity is the formation of the seed from the nutrients.

הנאכלת ובין החיה אשר לא תאכל, וסמיך ליה אשה כי תזריע, וסמך מצד אחר פרשת נגעים. ואלו הג' פרשיות לסודות נפלאים. ופרשה כי תזריע באמצע להודיע שאם יבדל אדם מן המאכלות הרעים הויין לו בנים הגונים קדושים וטהורים, ואם לאו הרי נגעים מתחדשים עליהם מצד טפת הזרע שהיתה מאותן מאכלות האסורות והמשוקצות.

ועל ידי כן בא להודיעך כי צריך האדם לקדש עצמו גם במאכלות הגונות סמוך לתשמיש כדי שיהיה מזרע נקי וטהור ובינוני בין צפון לדרום כמו שאמרנו. והנה הודענוך כי כפי המזון יהיה הדם הנולד, וכפי הדם יהיה הזרע, וכפי הזרע יהיה הולד הנולד ממנו. וכבר ידעת מה שאמרנו שלא יולד מן הסוס נשר ולא מן החטה עדשים, וכן נאמר כי לא יולד מן הזרע העכור והרע כי אם דם משוקץ ונתעב כאמרו (תהלים נח) זורו רשעים מרחם.

והנה הודענוך בדרך הזה דרך המזון הראוי. וראוי לנו לומר לך כי מן המזון הראוי אין צריך לקחת כדי מלוי הגוף רק דבר בינוני שיוכל הטבע לטחון אותו וימהר להתהפך לדם נקי וטהור, כי בהיות המאכל מתרבה באסטומכא אף על פי שיהיה מן הדברים ההגונים הנה רבויו יהיה גורם שלא יהיה נטחן ויפסד באצטומכא, ויהיה חוזר רע ומטונף יותר ממה שהיה מן [המעט אם יהיה מן] הדברים הגסים והרעים. לפיכך ראוי להזהר גם בשיעור המזון כאשר יזהר בגוף המזון ממש. הנה שמור זה העיקר הגדול שהוא ערוך מצד המזון לצד החבור.

Chapter Five

Intent and the Intimate Act

You must know the great secret that our rabbis of blessed memory said [*Yoma* 29a], that thoughts of sin can be more serious than the sin itself. I will enlighten you as to the deepest secrets of the world, which are hidden within rooms within rooms.

Understand that *Hashem* is the God of *dea* [knowledge, awareness], Who established His deeds with the purest wisdom, and gave in each aspect of nature an unchanging set of laws through miracles. He placed the potential in human beings to imagine and reproduce himself in the form of what he imagines, and it is natural for him to be aware of this. When a man has intimate relations with his wife, and his mind is occupied with thoughts and imaginings dealing with wisdom and understanding and good and proper behavior, that imagining in his thought has the potential to form a spiritual entity in the drop of seed resembling that imagining. This is the secret of Yaakov's manipulation of the offspring of his sheep with the striped sticks [*Bereishit* 30:37–39], as it says "The sheep were aroused by the sticks and the ewes gave birth to striped and spotted lambs."

Our rabbis woke us up to this [*Berachot* 20a] as Rabbi Yochanan went and sat at the gates of the *mikvah* so that the women leaving to go to their husbands would gaze upon him and have beautiful children resembling him spiritually. Consider

הדרך הרביעי - בכוונת החבור

צריך אתה לדעת מה שאז"ל סוד גדול (יומא כט א) קשה הרהור עבירה מעבירה. והנני מאיר עיניך בדברים שהם כבשונו של עולם והם נסתרים בכמה חדרים פנימים.

דע שהשם יתברך אל דעות התקין פעולותיו בחכמה תמימה ונתן כל טבע מטבעי העולם [כח] מיוחד פועל הדבר שניתן לו במשמרת מבלי שינוי רק בדרך נס. והנה נתן כח בדמיון האדם להוליד כיוצא בדבר שהוא מדמה. ודבר זה נדעהו גם מצד הטבע. והנה בהתחבר האדם אל אשתו, אם דמיונו ומחשבותיו עסוקים בחכמה ובינה ומדות טובות והגונות הנה אותו הדמיון אשר במחשבותיו, יש לו כח לצייר הצורה בטיפת הזרע כמו שהיה מדמה בשעת החבור, בלי ספק. וזהו סוד (בראשית ל) ויקח לו יעקב מקל לבנה וגו' ואומר ויחמו הצאן אל המקלות וגו'.

ורבותינו ז"ל אמרו בברכות (כא) רבי יוחנן הוה אזיל ויתיב אשערי טבילה אמר כי סלקן ואתיין בנות ישראל מנהרא לסתכלן בי כי היכי דלהוו להו זרעא שפירי כוותי. התבונן במראה הזה, כי זה החסיד הודיע כי בהיות האשה מחשבת ביפיו בעלותה מן הטבילה ומתחברת לבעלה, תחבר צורת הולד כפי הדמיון שהיא תדמה.

ואם כן נמצא הדמיון סבה גדול, וההרהור והמחשבה גורמין להיות הולד ומדותיו כאשר ביארנו, הנה שההרהור והמחשבה גורמין להיות

the great vision this pious man is presenting us. The woman going home from the *mikvah* would think about the visage of this beautiful and pious scholar and unite with her husband, and this thought in her imagination would give form to the *tzura* [form, spirituality] of the child she might conceive and his or her character, as we have explained.

Thus, thought causes the child to be righteous or wicked just as the food does. If so, every person must cleanse and purify his thoughts at the time of sexual relations and not be thinking sinful and licentious things, but rather the righteous, the pure, and the holy, for thoughts take form in the seed at the time of intimacy. Additionally, a man must make his wife comfortable and cause her and her heart to rejoice with words so that she is at one with him in the purity and clarity of thought and the matter of the *mitzvah*. Then their thoughts will be bound together as one, and the Divine Presence will dwell between them, and they will conceive offspring pure of spirit.

Do not be surprised, for an even greater fact in nature attests to the influence of thought. If a man is bitten by a rabid dog and he contracts the disease [hydrophobia], he cannot be given water, for he sees tiny rabid dogs in the water and in his urine. He is able to generate the tiny dogs in his urine with his thoughts!

Understand well the power of thought and imagination at the moment of the sex act. If a person thinks good and pure thoughts, those thoughts impinge on the drop of seed [zygote] and the offspring will be formed like that thought, say, to be a fully righteous person, about whom it is said, "Before I formed you in the womb, I knew you" [*Yirmiyahu* 1]. The good thought preceded the formation, then the Divine presence partnered with the pure thought, as the rabbis of blessed memory said, "The Holy One, blessed be He, combines a good thought with a deed" [*Kiddushin* 40a]. And if, Heaven forfend, a person thinks matters of sin and ugliness, the child will be founded on an evil foundation, destined to be evil, about whom it is said, "evil ones are estranged from the womb" [*Tehilim* 58].

הולד צדיק או רשע כאשר יגרום המזון כל זה. וצריך כל אדם לנקות מחשבותיו והרהוריו ולזכותם בשעת תשמיש, ולא יהיה מחשב בדבר עבירה וזמה רק בדברים הקדושים, ויהא מחשב בצדיקים הטהורים אנשי מדע והשכל וחכמה. כי אותן המחשבות יחולו על הזרע ויציירהו בצורתן בשעת תשמיש. וכן מחשבת אשתו. ושיהיה משמחה בדברים המשמחים את הלב כדי שתהיה גם היא מסכמת למחשבות זכות וטהורות, ויהיו שניהם אחדים בדבר המצוה, כי אז תתקשר מחשבתם לאחד ותהיה השכינה שרויה ביניהם, ויולידו בן כפי הצורה הטהורה שציירו.

ואל תתמה על דבר זה, כי טבע פשוט הוא בעיני חכמי המחקר, כי כפי המחשבה וההרהור שיעבור על לב האדם ואשתו בשעת חיבורם יהיה הולד מוכן ומצוייר אם טוב ואם רע. וכבר הביאו (מדרש תנחומא פ' נשא) מההיא מטרוניתא שילדה בן שחור והיתה היא והמלך לבנים יפים עד מאד וחשב המלך להרגה עד שבא חכם אחד וא"ל שמא הרהרה בשעת תשמיש באדם שחור ובדקו ומצאו צורות שחורות במשכיות אותו החדר ששמשה בו ואמרה כי היתה מסתכלת באותן הצורות ומהרהרת בהן בשעת החבור. וזהו כענין המקלות.

ואל תתמה, כי גדול מזה נודע בטבע, כי אדם שנשכו כלב שוטה וחלה חולי הידוע לאותה הנשיכה, הנה מאותה הדמיון שהוא מדמה ברעיוניו לא יוכלו להקריב לפניו מים, כי מיד ידמה לו שיש בהם כלבים שוטים, וגם בשתן שלו יראה דמיון כלבים [דקים] (רעים) עד מאד [ואם יסננו אותו השתן במסננת לא ימצאו בו שום דבר, אבל אם יתנו המים בכלי זכוכית ושהה שם שעה אחת יראו שם גורי הכלבים]. מפני רוב ההרהור והתמהון מצייר בשתן הרהוריו ותמהוניו.

והבן זה עד מאוד. וראה עד היכן כח המצייר וההרהור בשעת תשמיש. סוף דבר אדם מהרהר בדברים טובים וטהורים, הנה אותו ההרהור הטוב חל על טפת הזרע ויהיה הולד מצוייר כצורת אותו הרהור ועתיד להיות צדיק גמור, ועליו נאמר (ירמיה א) בטרם אצרך בבטן ידעתיך. ובאמת כי קודם הצורה שלו יהיה ההרהור הטוב מוכן לציירו, ואז השכינה משתתפת עם המחשבה הטהורה, כאמרם ז"ל (קידושין מ א) מחשבה טובה הקב"ה מצרפה למעשה. ואם אדם מחשב בדבר

The psalmist said [*Tehilim* 68:7], "God settles the solitary into families," which the rabbis explained [*Kiddushin* 70a] that if a man marries a woman for her beauty, he will enter a month and depart a month, and a sword will consume him, as it is written [*Hoshea* 5:7], "They betrayed *Hashem* for they had alien children, now a month [*Av*] will devour them." This is because if he married for beauty, his intimate act will not be for the sake of heaven but rather his thoughts will be toward her physical form and not her spirituality, and their offspring will be alien. That is, they caused the departure of the Divine Presence from between them due to the heat of their physicality. Their union became fire and fire [*alef shin*] without God [*yud heh*] between them – that is what is meant by "they betrayed *Hashem*."

To inform you of this message, the Torah approximates the portions of the "beautiful woman" and the "rebellious son" [*Devarim* 21].

You should know that not for naught did King David have problems with Avshalom, Amnon, and Tamar, all of whom were children of "beautiful women" from whose roots emerged similar branches, related to thoughts at conception.

I will transmit to you a great gift, the secret of thought and how it activates spirituality. Our rabbis said [*Kiddushin* 40a] that *Hashem* does not join evil thought and deed, with the exception of idolatry, as it is written [*Yechezkel* 14:5], "In order to seize the house of Israel for what is in their heart." Elsewhere they said [*Yoma* 29a] that sinful thoughts are harder than sinful deeds. I will enlighten you as to these sealed matters in Talmud. The rabbis said [*Vayikra Rabba* 16:4] Ben Azai would sit and learn and the fire would flame around him.[11] Rabbi Eliezer sat and interpreted and the rays that shone from him were like those of Moshe our teacher, of blessed memory. All these matters have one direction which I will clarify for you.

The wellspring drawn from a high place to a low place has the power to raise the water to another high place, as high as its pace of origin. Thus, it is known to the Kabbalists that a

עבירה וכיעור, הנה הולד מיוסד על יסוד רשע וכעור ועתיד להיות רשע מטונף, ועליו נאמר (תהלים נח) זורו רשעים מרחם.

ואני צריך לעוררך על יסוד גדול שבתורה ובדברי רבותינו ז"ל (תהלים סח, ז) אלהים מושיב יחידים ביתה, ואז"ל (קידושין ע א) כל הנושא אשה לשם יופי, חודש נכנס וחודש יוצא וחרב אוכלתו שנאמר (הושע ה) בה' בגדו כי בנים זרים ילדו עתה יאכלם חדש את חלקיהם. והסוד הגדול בזה, כי בהיותו נושא אשה לשם יופי, הרי חבורו אינו לשם שמים, כי אמנם הוא מהרהר בצורתה בדרך הגופניות ואינו מחשב במחשבה טהורה עליונה. והנה הבן הנולד מאותו הרהור הוא בן נכרי וזר, ועליו נאמר (הושע ה) כי בנים זרים ילדו, ואין לשם חלק בו. נמצאו בוגדים [לה', כלומר שגורמים לשכינה שתסתלק] (ושכינה מסתלקת) מביניהם. [נמצאו אש ואש ואין י - ה שרויה ביניהם. וזהו סוד בה' בגדו כי בנים זרים ילדו.]

ובאתי לעוררך עיקר גדול. דע כי לכך נסמכה פ' בן סורר ומורה ופרשת תלוי לפרשת יפת תואר, להודיע כי מאשה לקוחה בשביה לא יצא אדם צדיק. מאחר שאין הכוונה רק ליופי וזמה יצאו ממנה בנים סוררים ומורדים ראויים לארבע מיתות ב"ד.

ודע כי לא לחנם אירע לדוד ענין תמר ואמנון ואבשלום, כי שניהם בני יפת תואר היו. כי כל זה גורם ההרהור כיוצא באותה הצורה. ואם כן בין במה שעוררנוך בפרק זה בענין כוונת החבור והמחשבה וההרהור.

ואני רוצה לעוררך על עיקר גדול, ואמסור לך מתנה גדולה בסוד המחשבה היאך היא פועלת הצורה בדבר שהיא נתקבלה ממנו. הנה רבותינו ז"ל אמרו (יומא כט א) הרהורי עבירה קשים מעבירה, ובמקום אחר אמרו (קידושין מ א) מחשבה רעה אין הקדוש ב"ה מצרפה למעשה חוץ מע"א שנאמר (יחזקאל יד) למען תפוש את בית ישראל בלבם. והנני מאיר עיניך בדברים סתומים באו בגמרא. הנה אז"ל (ויקרא רבה טז, ד) בן עזאי היה יושב ושונה והיתה האש מלהטת סביבותיו ורבי אלעזר יושב ודורש וקרנותיו יוצאות כקרנותיו של משה רבינו ע"ה. ותצטרך לדעת כי כל אלו הדברים כוונה אחת להם, והנני מבאר.

---

11. Recanati, *Tetze*: Through the cleaving of his thought to the supernal realm, a fire descended from heaven as he dealt with the holy chariot.

man's thoughts drawn from the spiritual soul are drawn from the supernatural realm. Thought has the potential to spread and rise and reach the place of its original source. Then it will cleave to the supernal secret from which it was drawn and thought and supernal secret will become one. When thought returns from above to below, it takes the form of a single line, whose light is drawn down by the power of thought, and then the light of clarity [*habahir*] is drawn and spreads to the place where the thinker sits. This is the secret of Elisha's cruse of oil and Eliyahu's pitcher of flour [*Melachim I*, 17 and *Melachim II*, 4]. When a man unites with his wife and their thoughts cleave to the supernal realm, the supernal light is drawn down to reside on the drop [zygote] that they were thinking about, like Elisha's cruse, and that drop is tied together forever with the light of clarity. This is the secret of "as I formed you in the womb, I knew you," for the light of clarity was tied to the drop of the righteous one at the moment of conception.

Understand this well, and from it you will understand the great secret of the God of Avraham, the God of Yitzchak, and the God of Yaakov. The secret is that their thoughts were never separated from the Supernal Light, even for a moment. The patriarchs were like slaves owned by the aster forever. At the time they were involved in eating, drinking, intimacy, and other bodily pursuits, words of Torah were with them and all their intention was for the Name of Heaven. On account of this, Yaakov merited to have twelve tribes, each completely pure and righteous, fitting to be bearers of Hashem's vessels, for their thoughts were Supernal Light even when they had marital relations.[12]

Out of this, Yaakov our father merited to produce twelve tribes, all purely righteous, bearers of the vessels of *Hashem*, for their thoughts were never separate from cleaving to the supernal, even during intimacy.

Shlomo said [*Mishlei* 3:6], "In all your ways, know Him, and He will straighten your paths." The rabbis said, in all your ways,

כי מעין המים בהיותו נמשך ממקום גבוה למקום נמוך, יש כח להעלות אותם המים אל מקום אחר גבוה כנגד גובה המים שיוצאין ממנו. וכן ידוע לבעלי הקבלה כי מחשבת האדם היא ממקור הנפש השכלית שנמשכה מן העליונים, ויש כח במחשבה להתפשט ולעלות ולהגיע עד מקום מוצאה, ובהגיע אל המקור אז היא נדבקה בסוד העליון, שמשם נמשכת ונעשית היא והוא דבר אחד. וכשהמחשבה חוזרת להמשך ממעלה למטה, נעשה הכל כדמיון קו אחד ואותו האור העליון נמשך למטה בכח המחשבה שמושכת אותה למטה [ונמצאת שכינה למטה] ואז האור הבהיר נמשך ומתפשט באותו המקום שבעל המחשבה יושב שם. וכן היו חסידים הראשונים מדבקין מחשבתן בעליונים ומושכין האור העליון למטה ומתוך כך היו הדברים מתוספין ומתרבין כפי כח המחשבה. וזהו סוד השמן של אלישע עליו השלום וכד הקמח וצפחת השמן של אליהו.

ואחר שהדבר כן, הוצרכו רבותינו ז"ל לומר כי בהתחבר האדם לאשתו ומחשבתו נדבקת בעליונים, הרי אותה המחשבה מושכת אור עליון למטה והוא שורה על אותה טפה שהוא מתכוין עליה ומהרהר בה, כענין הצפחת, ונמצאת אותה טפה נקשרת לעולם באור הבהיר. וזהו סוד בטרם אצרך בבטן ידעתיך, מפני שכבר נקשר האור הבהיר בטפת אותו צדיק בעת החבור לפי שהמחשבה נקשרת בעליונים, ומשכה האור הבהיר.

והבן זה עד מאד. ותבין ממנו סוד גדול בענין אלהי אברהם אלהי יצחק ואלהי יעקב. [כי זהו הסוד, שלא היה מחשבתם נפרדת אפילו שעה אחת ורגע אחד מן האור העליון. ונמצאו האבות כעבדים הקנויים לאדון קנין עולם, ולפיכך אמר אלהי אברהם אלוהי יצחק ואלוהי יעקב.] ושם נאמר כי בעת שהיו עוסקים במאכל ובמשתה ובמשגל ובשאר עסקי הגוף, דברי תורה מה תהא עליהם, והיתה התשובה כי גם בכל עסקי הגוף כל כוונתם היתה לשם שמים. ולא היתה מחשבתם נפרדת מן האור העליון אפילו רגע אחד. ומתוך כך זכה יעקב להוליד י"ב שבטים כלם צדיקים גמורים ותמימים היו, וראויין להיות כדמיון סדרי

12. See Rambam, Laws of *Deot*, 3:2 and Ramban, *Devarim* 22:11.

even your small and large bodily needs, "Know Him" means the connection with the spiritual soul and the cleaving with the supernal light. Just as the union of man and wife is called *yedia* [knowledge], the cleaving of the soul to the supernal realm is called *yedia*.

Now let us consider why sinful thoughts are harder than sinful deeds. When a person thinks about evil and filthy ways his thoughts are in a filthy state above and his soul is guilty to the heavens, for he has contaminated it. But the sinful deeds have a lesser effect, their judgment does not reach the heavens, and compared to sinful thoughts, sinful deeds are easier for him. Thoughts have their roots above, and if their consequence is a cut, that cut will be close to the root. If he has a sinful thought at the time of intimacy, the filth of that thought will contaminate the drop and establish from it an evil, crooked, filthy foundation, called "alien." Now you can understand the importance of Rabbi Yochanan sitting at the gate of the *mikvah*.

Speaking of thoughts, there is something else you must know. The thoughts and intentions of the pious become fulfilled, for good or for bad. This is why when the sage cast his eye upon a person, that person became a pile of bones [*Bava Basra* 75a], and another sage said, "Return to your dust" [*Taanit* 24a], and "Wherever the sages cast their eyes, either death or poverty resulted" [*Chagigah* 5b].

This is the subject matter of prayer and sacrifice, the secret of cleaving to the supernal realm. From this matter is derived the power of the cursed Bilaam, about whom they said [*Bamidbar* 22:6], "Whomever you bless is blessed, and whomever you curse is cursed." He wanted to carefully inspect Israel in order to cleave his thoughts to the supernal and draw wicked thoughts upon them, so he "raised his eyes and saw Israel residing according to their tribes" [*Bamidbar* 24:2]. Connecting his thoughts to the upper realm, he drew supernal power to the intended target, and this is what is meant by [*Bamidbar* 24:4] " he saw that he had seen enough." This is the reason for the seven altars, the bullock

עולם נושאי כלי ה׳, לפי שלא היתה מחשבתם נפרדת מהאור העליון אפילו בשעת החבור.

ולכן אמר שלמה ע״ה (משלי ג) בכל דרכיך דעהו, [אמרו חז״ל (ברכות סג ב) בכל דרכיך דעהו אפ׳ לכל צרכי הגוף קטן וגדול. ומה שאמר דעהו כבר ידעת] ידיעה זו היא חבור הנפש השכלית ודבוקה באור העליון [כאשר חבור האדם באשה נקרא ידיעה, כן דבוק הנפש בעולם השכל נקרא ידיעה, וכבר ידעת שלא] (ולא) נקרא האדם יודע דבר פלוני עד שנדבק המשכיל במושכל. [והבן זה מאד. א״כ התבונן סוד אומרו בכל דרכיך דעהו, וסמיך ליה והוא יישר ארחותיך, כי האור העליון יהיה נדבק במעשיו ויהיו כולם בסדר נכון וקיים. וזהו מאמר חז״ל (אבות פ״ב מי״ב) וכל מעשיך יהיו לש״ש.]

ואחר שהודענוך זה, התבונן בהיות הרהורי עבירה קשים מעבירה, כי בהיות אדם מחשב בדברי רשע וטנוף מחשבתו נדבקת בטנופה בעליונים, והרי נפשו מחוייבת לשמים שהרי היא מטמאה במגע, אבל אלו עשה עבירה למטה ולא נגע משפטה לשמים, יקל מעליו יותר מהרהור הרע [שהוא נדבק בעליונים] והוא קרוב לקצץ בנטיעות. ומכאן תבין סוד מהרהר עבירה בשעת תשמיש כי אותה המחשבה המטונפת חלה על הטפה ומיסדה ממנה יסוד רשע ועול וטנוף, ונקראת זרה. [והבן זה אם בעל נפש אתה.] ומכאן תבין מעשה של אותו חסיד שהיה יושב בשערי טבילה כדי שתהיין מחשבתן והרהורם נדבקת בצורתו, וצורתו נקשרת בעליונים.

ועוד נודיע לך ענין אחר בענין המחשבה, אף על פי שאינו מכוונת החבור, עם כל זה הוא מועיל לו ולזולתו. והוא, כי בהיות החסידים הקדושים מדביקים מחשבתם בעליונים, כל דבר שמחשבין עליו באותה שעה היה מתקיים אם טוב ואם רע. והוא שאמרו (ב״ב עה א) נתן עיניו בו ונעשה גל של עצמות. וכתוב בתענית (כד א) בההיא ברתא תובי לעפרך, וכן היה. ומה שאמרו (חגיגה ה ב) כל מקום שנתנו חכמים עיניהם בו או מיתה או עוני.

ומהענין הזה סוד התפלה והקרבנות, שהוא סוד דבוק בעליונים. ומהענין הזה היה כח אותו ארור בלעם הרשע, שהיו אומרים עליו את אשר תברך מבורך ואשר תאור יואר. ולפיכך היה רוצה לעיין בישראל עיון שלם כדי שיוכל להדביק מחשבתו בעליונים וימשיך עליהם מחשבה

and ram on each to complete all the powers and bring them close to his thought to fulfill his evil wish. However, *Hashem*, who knows and understands all thoughts, took the measure of his evil thought and obliterated it, and left nothing to the will of the wicked Bilaam but only to His will, may He be blessed. If you understand this you will see the degree to which the power of thought reaches, for good or for bad. Now apply this to the power of thought at the time of the intimate act.

MDK: While previous chapters dealt metaphorically with physiological principles of digestion and reproduction, this one deals with sechel, the work of the mind as it relates to sexuality. Sechel has two meanings and both are intended: intellect and spirituality. The work product of the intellect – thought – drives and energizes the deeds of man, for good or for better. The same deed, e.g. the intimate act, is framed and structured by thought to be sacred or profane, and the resultant offspring are similarly affected.

רעה. ולפיכך אמר (במדבר כד) וישא בלעם את עיניו וירא את ישראל שוכן לשבטיו. ולפיכך הוצרך לדקדק (שם כב) לך נא אתי אל מקום אחר אשר תראנו משם וגו׳, כי הרשע היה צריך לעיין במה שכוונתו עליו, לטוב או לרע, והיה מדביק מחשבתו למעלה, והיה מושך כח עליון למי שהיה מתכוין ומעיין בו. וזהו ענין (שם כד) מחזה שדי יחזה נופל וגלוי עינים. ולפיכך נתכוין הרשע לבנות המזבחות שבעה ופר ואיל בכל אחד, כדי להכנים אליו כל הכחות ולקרבם אל מחשבתו, כדי לקיים חפצו ורצונו הרע בכל אשר יאוה. ולזה אמר (במדבר כג) ויקחהו שדה צופים, שהיה הרשע צופה בהם כדי להמשיך עליהם מחשבתו הרעה. אבל הקדוש ב״ה שיודע כל המחשבות ידע מחשבתו הרעה, ולא הניחה לרצונו של בלעם הרשע. והבן זה מאד ותדע עד היכן מגיע כח המחשבה. [ואע״פ שאין זה מכוונת הספר, תועיל לך בו תועלת שלמה בהיותך יודע שעור ההרהור עד היכן נוגע, ותדע סוד המחשבה מה היא פועלת בשעת החבור.]

ואחר שהודענוך סודות אלו הסתומים יש לנו להודיעך סוד הדרך הסמוך לזה, כפי הראוי, בעז״ה:

Chapter Six

The Quality of the Intimate Act

It is well known that any pious and modest person speaks softly, with gentle and comfortable language without overstatement, and walks modestly with head bent and eyes down. The evil person does just the opposite. We have discussed that while no part of a person's body can be deprecated, its actions can. Therefore, at all times you and your wife are intimate, do not behave with lightheartedness, speaking nonsense and foolishness, and do not have too much vain conversation with her. Therefore, you must first engage her with words that draw upon her heartstrings and settle her mind, and cause her to rejoice, in order that her consciousness is bound to your consciousness, and her intent to your intent. Speak some words designed to arouse desire and connection and love and willingness, and some words that draw her to fear of heaven and piety and modesty. Relate to her how modest, pious women bear proper, pure children, fitting for the lofty crown, possessors of Torah and fear of *Hashem*, and great, holy people of good deeds, like Kimchit, who merited having seven sons who served as high priests. When she was asked how she merited this, she said that the walls of her house never saw the braids of her hair [*Yerushalmi Megilah* 1:12]. Converse with her at midnight or toward the last third of the night [*Berachot* 3a]. Do not force yourself upon her, for a sexual act like that, not done with mutual desire and love and willingness, does not

[כבר הודענוך בפרקים אלו דברים רבים שיש לך לכלול אותם עם מה שנאמר בפרק זה. ושימם כחותם על לבך. והנני מתחיל ואומר] ידוע כי כל איש חסיד וצנוע, כשהוא מדבר, אינו מדבר כי אם בלשון רכה ושפה רפה ובנחת רוח, ואינו מדבר גדולות, וכשהוא מהלך ילך בקומה כפופה וראשו נמוך, וכן בכל מנהגיו. והרשע בכל דרכיו בחפף מזח. ואתה יש לך לעיין [אם יש לך עיניים לראות], כי מאחר שהדברים שאין להם גנות אבר אצל בני אדם, יש להם גנות מעשה וענין רע, כל שכן בדברים שיש בהם גנות אבר אצל בני אדם כל שכן גנות אבר וגנות מעשה. ועל כן, כל זמן שהאדם מתחבר לאשה, אל יהא בקלות ראש ודברי שוא ותעתועים, ואל תקל ראשך כנגד האשה, ואל תרבה בשיחה בטלה עמה. ולפיכך יש לך להכניסה תחלה בדברים שמושכין את לבה ומיישבין דעתה ומשמחין אותה, כדי שתקשר דעתה בדעתך וכוונתה בכוונתך. תאמר לה דברים קצתם מכניסין אותה בדברי חשק ואהבה ורצון, וקצתם מושכין אותה ליראת שמים וחסידות וצניעות. ומספר עמה בדברי נשים חסידות וצנועות, היאך יצאו מהם בנים הגונים וכשרים, ראויים לכתר עליון, בעלי תורה ויראה והוראה, כמעשה קמחית שזכתה לז' בנים שכולם שמשו בכהונה גדולה, ושאלוה חכמינו ז"ל במה זכתה, ואמרה להם אפילו קורות ביתי לא ראו שער ראשי מימי, וכל זה הפליגה לשאר

have the Divine Presence dwelling within it. Do not enter her while she is asleep for such an act would lack her agreement, but it is proper to wake her up with words of endearment. It is improper to fight with her about intimacy. But it is proper to draw out her heart with words of grace and seduction to reach a mutual intent for the sake of heaven. In summary, when you sense the time is right for intimacy with your wife, do it such that her *daat* is in agreement with yours.

Do not be quick to arouse your desire, but make her comfortable so that she can enter a state of love and willingness, to be able to cast her seed first, for her *chomer* to be ready for your *tzura* to act upon it. Your intention should not be only for the pleasure of intercourse, but the fulfillment of the obligation and *mitzvah* to sexually gratify your wife as it says in the Torah. Consider the big picture, how a pious person directs his lofty intention and your deed will be for the sake of heaven, a complete *mitzvah.*

Beyond the modesty with which one conducts himself in all his other affairs, his act of intimacy requires special thought, which imprints spirituality upon the drop of seed.

This is the secret of [*Bereishit* 25:19] "These are the generations of Yitzchak the son of Avraham, Avraham bore Yitzchak." This means that upon hearing that Sara would have a son with whom *Hashem* would establish a covenant, Avraham directed his intent during intimacy with Sara to the supernal realm – this is how he "bore" Yitzchak. This *tzadik ben tzadik* had no internal or external defect, and this is the secret of his being brought up as a sacrifice. The kind of sacrifice, *ola*, is brought for thoughts of the heart [*Vayikra Rabba*, 63:1].[13] His perfection was the result of the purity of his father's thoughts at the moment of conception.

This matter pertains to all pious, soulful people, whose intent is for the sake of *mitzvah,* who cleave their consciousness and thought at the time of intimacy to the supernal and bear children fitting for holiness, purity, and caring. "And these are the generations of Peretz. Peretz bore Chetzron… and Yishai

צניעותה וחסידותה ויושר מעשיה. [ויכנים אותה בדברים אלו, מהם אהבים ומהם עגבים, ומהם יראת שמים וצניעות וטוהר מחשבה.]

ויספר עמה באמצע הלילה או סמוך לשליש האחרון, דתניא בברכות (ג א) משמרה שלישית תינוק יונק משדי אמו ואשה מספרת עם בעלה. [וכשהוא בועל אותה, לא יבעלנה בעל כרחה ולא יאנוס אותה, מפני שאותו החבור אין השכינה שורה בו מפני שכוונתו בהפך מכוונתה ואין דעת אשתו מוסכמת לדעתו. ולא יריבנה ולא יכה אותה על עסקי תשמיש. והנה אמרו רז"ל במסכת יומא (פסחים מט ב) מה ארי דורס ואוכל ואין לו בושת פנים אף עם הארץ מכה ובועל ואין לו בושת פנים. אבל הוי מושך לבה בדברי חן ופתוי ושאר דברים הגונים ומחושבים. ואל תהי בועל אותה והיא ישנה, מפני שאין כוונת שניכם אחדות ואין מחשבתה מוסכמת אל מחשבתך, אבל הוי מעורר אותה ומכניסה בדברים]. סוף דבר, כשתהיה בודק בעצמך ותראה שאתה ראוי לשמש, עשה שתהיה דעת אשתך מוסכמת לדעתך.

וכשאתה מתחבר עמה אל תמהר לעורר בה התאוה, כדי שתתישב דעתה, [ותכנס עמה בדרך אהבה ורצון, בענין שתזריע היא תחלה, כדי שיהיה הזרע שלה כחומר והזרע שלך כצורה, כענין שנאמר אשה כי תזריע וילדה זכר. וכבר ידעת מה שאמרו (נדרים כ ב) בענין אותו חסיד שאמרה אשתו עליו שהיה מגלה טפח ומכסה טפחיים ודומה כמי שכפאו שד, כלומר שלא היה מתכוון להנאת תשמיש לבד, אלא שהיה בעיניו כמי שמתעסק בדבר אחר שאינו ממלאכתו אלא שהוא חוב מוטל עליו לגמרו משום מצות עונה האמורה בתורה. והתבונן ותראה האיך היה זה החסיד מתכוין כונה עליונה, שכל מעשהו היה לשם שמים ולמצוה גמורה.]

ומכל הדברים שהודענוך בפרקים הקודמים ובזה הפרק, יש לך להקיש כמה דברים שלא זכרנו מן הדברים שזכרנו, והוי כולל כל הדברים כלם. ומדעתך תבין דרך ההנהגה שהאדם ראוי להתנהג בה בשעת תשמיש יותר מכל צניעות שאתה צנוע על כל מדותיך, במאכל

13. Recanati, Vayikra: Ola, the remedy for forbidden thoughts, requires flaying, cutting and burning whole and complete, soul as well as flesh, returning it all to ruach [spirit, wind].

bore David" [*Rut* 4:18–22]. Not for nothing did *Hashem* choose David king of Israel, but he was part of a chain of totally righteous forebears, one after the other, one above the other, comparable to the Ten Orders of the World [*Sefirot*], in the secret of *yud* that includes all. When you conduct yourself as I have informed you, I guarantee you will have pious, righteous children, who sanctify *Hashem's* Name.

And God in His mercy will open our eyes to the light of His Torah and merit us to reach His reaching of the secrets of His Torah, and have children prepared to fear and serve Him. Amen and Amen.

ובמשתה ובדרך ארץ. כי כפי הצניעות ומחשבה שאתה נוהג בשעת החבור כך תחול הצורה על טפת הזרע.

וזהו סוד (בראשית כה) ואלה תולדות יצחק בן אברהם אברהם הוליד את יצחק, כלומר אחר שאמר ליה הקב"ה שרה אשתך יולדת לך בן, נתכוין אברהם בשעת החבור כוונה יתרה על כל מדותיו הטובות, בהיותו מדבק מחשבתו בעליונים ומתכוין להוליד בן שיהיה ראוי למה שאמר לו הקדוש ב"ה. וזהו סוד אברהם הוליד את יצחק, נתכוין להוליד בן שיהיה צדיק גמור כמותו. וזהו אלה תולדות יצחק בן אברהם, אז"ל (בראשית רבה סג א) צדיק בן צדיק. והגיע כח צדקו עד שהעיד הקדוש ב"ה שאין בו מום, לא בפנים ולא בחוץ. וזהו סוד ויעלהו שם לעולה, וכבר ידעת שלא היה ראוי שיהיה מום בדבר הקרב על גבי המזבח. הבן המראה הגדול הזה. וכבר ידעת כי העולה היא קודש קדשים, והיא באה על הרהור הלב וחטאות המורגשות, ולפיכך צריכה הפשט ונתוח [וכליל לשמים], ונקרא יצחק עולה תמימה. וכל זה גרם אותו אברהם בשעת החבור שנתכוון לשם שמים ממש.

וכן הדבר נוהג בשאר החסידים אנשי לבב, כי בהתכוונם לשם מצוה להדביק מחשבתם בעליונים בשעת החבור, אז יולידו בנים ראויים לקדושה ולטהרה ולחסידות. ולפיכך הוצרכה מגילת רות לכתוב (רות ד) ואלה תולדות פרץ פרץ הוליד את חצרון, כאשר פרץ צדיק גמור נתכוין גם הוא להוליד בן צדיק כמותו, וזהו סוד פרץ הוליד את חצרון. וכן חצרון נתכוין גם הוא להוליד בן צדיק כמותו, וזהו סוד חצרון הוליד את רם. וכן עד ישי הוליד את דוד, צדיק בן צדיק. להודיע כי לא על חנם בחר הקדוש ב"ה בדוד עבדו, כי שלשלת עשרה צדיקים גמורים זה למעלה מזה, כדמיון עשרה סדרי עולם [בסוד שעור קומה] בסוד יו"ד [שהכל כלול בה. ולפיכך נקרא דוד ביו"ד על עשר מעלות כלולות בו], כי מפרץ ועד דוד עשר מעלות, צדיק בן צדיק. ועתה התבונן סוד מה שכללנו בדברים אלו. וכשתהיה נוהג בהם כמה שהודעתיך, אני ערב לך להוליד בן צדיק וחסיד מקדש שם שמים.

[והש"י ברחמיו יפקח עינינו במאור תורתו, יזכנו להשיג השגתו מסודות תורתו, ולהוליד בנים מוכנים ליראתו ולעבודתו, אמן ואמן.]

About the Translator

Dr. Moshe David Kuhr, a native of Dayton, Ohio, attended Yeshivas Chofetz Chaim of Baltimore and earned his medical degree from the University of Chicago. After 43 years of pediatric practice, he made *aliyah* with his wife, Phyllis, to Jerusalem, where he dedicates his time to learning, teaching and writing. His Torah mentors include Rabbis Boruch Milikovsky *z"l*, Berel Wein *z"l*, Moshe Tendler *z"l*, Avraham Pessin *z"l*, Yaacov Haber, Dr. Yehuda Eliezri, and more recently, Yitzchak Breitowitz. He attributes his broad Torah knowledge to the guidance of these mentors and to numerous *chavrutot*. Dr. Kuhr's accomplishments include four books on the works of the Maharal of Prague (*Lion Club of Prague Bereshit*, *Lion Club of Prague Shemot and Vayikra*, *Lion Club of Prague Bamidbar and Devarim*, and *Paths of the Maharal*) – three on *Gur Arye*, a commentary on Rashi on the Torah, and one on *Netivot Olam*.

Dr. Kuhr's interest in the dispersed communities of Israel has led him on five trips to India and the former Soviet Union. The Kuhrs have, *b'ezrat Hashem*, four sons, three of whom have made *aliyah*, and twelve grandchildren, including three serving in the Israel Defense Forces.